I0813991

TOAST

To Justin and Ted, Mum and Dad – my guinea pigs, my champions and my cheerleaders. Thank you for your unwavering support. And Justin, for sampling seven meals a day, always with a smile.

Design by Georgie Hewitt
Props supplied by Max Robinson

Published in 2025 by OH
An Imprint of HEADLINE PUBLISHING GROUP LIMITED

1

Cataloguing in Publication Data is available from the British Library

ISBN 978-1-03542-074-2

Printed and bound in China by C&C Offset Printing Co., Ltd.

Headline's policy is to use papers that are natural, renewable and recyclable products and made from wood grown in well-managed forests and other controlled sources. The logging and manufacturing processes are expected to conform to the environmental regulations of the country of origin.

HEADLINE PUBLISHING GROUP LIMITED
An Hachette UK Company
Carmelite House
50 Victoria Embankment
London EC4Y 0DZ

The authorised representative in the EEA is Hachette Ireland, 8 Castlecourt Centre, Castleknock Road, Castleknock, Dublin 15, D15 YF6A, Ireland (email: info@hbgi.ie)

www.headline.co.uk
www.hachette.co.uk

TOAST

80 Delicious Recipes for Toast with a Twist

Katie Marshall

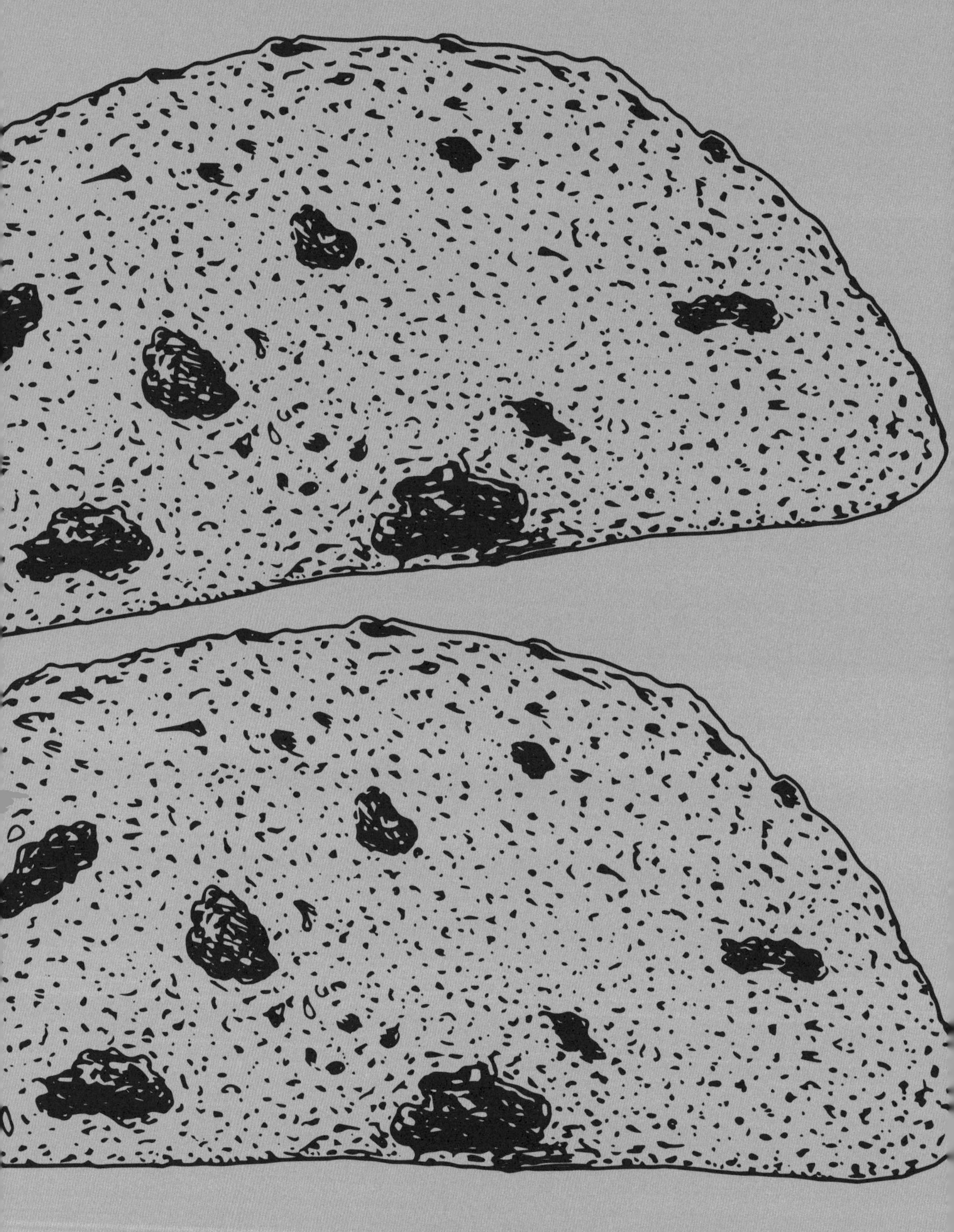

Contents

Introduction

This book is a celebration of all the things I've found to be perfect to round up into a delicious meal by being delicately presented – or even indelicately plonked – on a steaming, golden, aromatic slice of toast.

The refuge of the diner who has run out of time, imagination or inclination, everyone has succumbed at one time or another to a simple poached egg, a shower of cheese or a flood of hot beans on toast – or just toast spread with butter and jam – and there's nothing wrong with that. But we can do better, and here is a collection of recipes to expand the horizons of your toast-based feasting.

I've taken inspiration from countries I've travelled to and restaurants I've eaten at to bring you this selection of recipes which will take you from breakfast through to dessert, via the dips and spreads aisle, and with a tour of the cheese counter. I've even managed to completely sully the integrity of spaghetti carbonara by piling my interpretation onto some toasted ciabatta (and I'm definitely not sorry about it). There's a dish for every occasion: snacks to be relished alone on the sofa; meals that will give amazing leftovers for the next day's lunch; dishes to share with friends and family; and even meals for special occasions that will have your guests begging for the recipe. There's something for everyone – particularly the solo diner who has run out of the energy to keep on thinking up simple but nutritious and appetizing new ideas. And we shouldn't forget that there's a chapter of easy desserts for when you just need a little something sweet to finish off your meal.

I've offered serving suggestions for which type of bread might maximize on the flavours of each dish, but you'll have your own favourites so feel free to mix and match depending on what's in the bread box, or what suits your taste.

I hope some of these recipes will be added to your repertoire and will be as much of a joy for you to eat as they have been for me to write! I've been working in the food world for nearly 15 years and have become a connoisseur of fridge-raids and cannily using up leftovers – these whipped-up meals often finding their home on a piece of bread – so this is finally my chance to make toast the star!

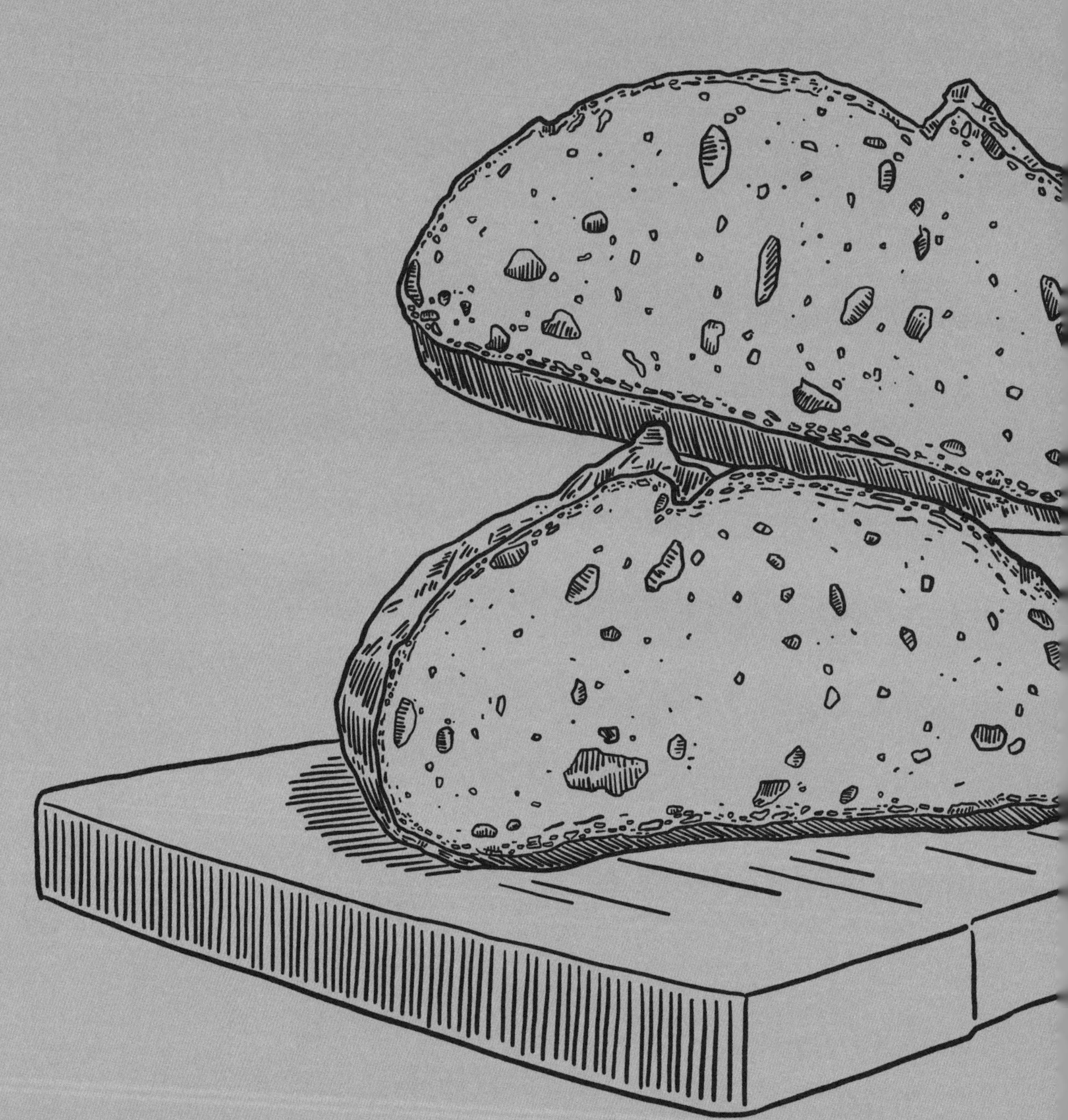

Toasting Breads

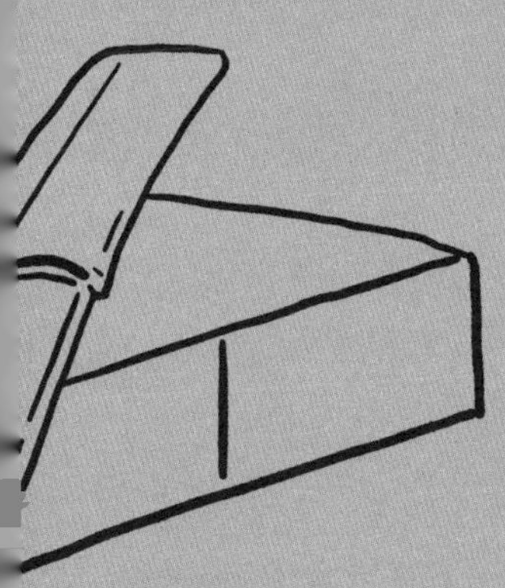

Melba toast

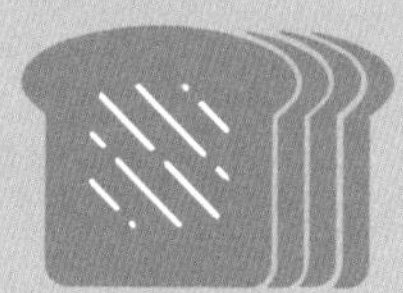

SERVES **4**

PREPARATION TIME **10 MINUTES**

COOKING TIME **8–10 MINUTES**

Melba toast is the name given to dry, crisp, thin pieces of toast! Perfect with pâté, mousses or cheese, they're a crunchy vessel for loading up with deliciousness. They are also an easy and economical way of using up slightly stale bread and will keep in an airtight container for up to a week.

4 slices of medium sliced white bread

Preheat the oven to 160°C fan (350°F/gas 4) and prepare two baking sheets, lining one with baking parchment.

Lightly toast the bread in a toaster until golden. Leave to cool, then remove the crusts. Use a bread knife to carefully cut through each slice, splitting it into two very thin slices. Place toasted-side down on a work surface and lightly roll the bread with a rolling pin to flatten it. Cut each piece in half, so each piece of bread has now made four rectangles.

Place on the lined baking sheet, toasted-side down. Cover with the second baking sheet so the pieces are all covered.

Cook for 8–10 minutes until all the pieces of bread are evenly golden brown all over, turning the tray halfway through to make sure the colour is even.

Brioche

MAKES **1 LARGE LOAF**

PREPARATION TIME **15 MINUTES, PLUS 3½ HOURS PROVING**

COOKING TIME **50 MINUTES**

This loaf is the answer to most of your toasted-dessert treats (and some epic savoury combinations, too). The smell of the butter is so sweet and intoxicating – reminiscent of stacks of croissants in a Parisian bakery.

500g (1lb 2oz) strong white bread flour
2 tsp table salt
60g (2¼oz) golden caster sugar
7g (¼oz) sachet of dried active yeast
120ml (4fl oz) whole milk
5 eggs, plus 1 for egg wash
210g (7½oz) salted butter, at room temperature, cubed

For the Brioche with Ricotta and Jam recipe in the image overleaf, see page 150

Put the flour, salt, sugar and yeast in the bowl of a stand mixer. Put the milk in a small saucepan over a low heat and heat until warm. Using the dough hook, start to mix the dry ingredients together, then slowly add the milk, followed by the eggs, and mix for 8–10 minutes until glossy and combined.

Add the butter, a couple of cubes at a time, then run the mixer on high for about 5 minutes until all the ingredients are incorporated and the dough is glossy and quite loose. Transfer to a lightly greased bowl, cover and leave to rise for about 2 hours, or until doubled in size. Refrigerate for 1 hour.

Grease and line a 2kg (4lb 8oz) sized loaf tin. Turn the dough out onto a lightly floured surface and knock the air out. Divide into 9 and shape into balls, then place them on the base of the loaf tin. Cover with clingfilm (plastic wrap) again and leave to prove for another 30 minutes.

Meanwhile, preheat the oven to 160°C fan (350°F/gas 4).

Bake for 50 minutes until golden and the space in the seams of the balls feels firm to the touch. Cool in the tin for 30 minutes before transferring to a wire rack to cool completely.

Date and caraway soda bread

MAKES **1 MEDIUM LOAF**

PREPARATION TIME **5 MINUTES**

COOKING TIME **50 MINUTES**

This super-speedy loaf has no yeast, so has no proving time and limited intimidation potential. Sweetened with dates and lightly spiced with anise-tasting caraway, this bread is good fresh or toasted and can be paired with sweet or savoury toppings.

250g (9oz) wholemeal flour
250g (9oz) strong bread flour
1 tsp bicarbonate of soda
1 tsp flaky sea salt
2 tbsp golden caster sugar
1 tbsp caraway seeds, toasted and lightly crushed in a pestle and mortar
100g (3½oz) medjool dates, pitted and roughly chopped
300ml (10fl oz) buttermilk
150ml (5fl oz) milk

Preheat the oven to 180°C fan (375°F/gas 5) and line a baking sheet with baking parchment.

Combine the flours, bicarbonate of soda, salt, sugar, caraway seeds and dates in a bowl. Mix the milk and buttermilk in a jug, then very quickly mix it into the dry mixture using a spatula. Shape the dough into a ball, then transfer to the prepared baking sheet. Use a sharp knife to make a cross shape in the top.

Bake for 50 minutes until risen and golden, then leave to cool for 5 minutes before transferring to a wire rack to cool completely.

Sourdough loaf

MAKES **1 MEDIUM LOAF**

PREPARATION TIME **30 MINUTES, PLUS LOTS OF RESTING**

COOKING TIME **45 MINUTES**

Along with the rest of the world, I got sucked into the ritual of sourdough-making during the Covid-19 pandemic – adhering to a daily routine of twisting and turning my sticky dough project. Real life doesn't allow me to nurture a loaf every day, but I bring my starter out of the fridge when I know I have an occasion coming up and I want really delicious homemade bread. For those who haven't tried sourdough before, I've provided instructions for the essential sourdough starter.

FOR THE SOURDOUGH STARTER

100g (3¾oz) rye flour

125ml (4fl oz) lukewarm water

EACH DAY

50g (2oz) rye flour

50g (2oz) plain flour

115ml (4¼fl oz) lukewarm water

FOR THE LOAF

100g (3½oz) sourdough starter

350g (12oz) strong bread flour, plus extra for dusting

150g (5oz) rye flour or strong bread flour, if preferred

325–350ml (11–12fl oz) warm water

3 tsp flaky sea salt

To begin a starter from scratch, combine 100g rye flour with 125ml lukewarm water in a wide-based jam jar. Mix well with a plastic spatula, then cover the top of the jar with a piece of muslin or a clean tea towel and leave somewhere warm for 24 hours.

The next day, combine 75g (3oz) of your mixture with 50g rye flour, 50g plain flour and 115ml (4¼fl oz) of lukewarm water in a small bowl. Discard the rest of your day one starter and put your new mixture back into your cleaned jar. Cover, and leave for another 24 hours, as before.

Repeat the process every day for a week. You should now notice that your mixture becomes bubbly and elasticated, rising up the sides of your jar. It's now ready to use! If you are making bread regularly, you should feed it daily; otherwise you can refrigerate your mixture, then bring it to room temperature and feed it for a few days before you want to make a loaf of sourdough.

To make the loaf, combine the starter and flour(s) in a large bowl, then mix in 325ml warm water with your hand until the mixture resembles scraggy porridge. Add a little more water if necessary or if you are happy with a wetter dough. Cover with a clean tea towel and set aside for 1 hour.

CONTINUED OVERLEAF

Sprinkle the dough with the salt and poke holes into it with your index finger, then set aside for 15 minutes.

With wet hands, pull the dough up from the far side of the bowl and stretch it over to the near side. Turn the bowl 45 degrees and repeat. By stretching the dough like this, the gluten will begin to develop. Do this 8 times (until your bowl has travelled a full circle). Cover and set aside for 20 minutes, then repeat the process 3 more times. Cover the bowl and leave for 3 hours.

Tip the dough onto a floured surface (or moistened with water if you're confident with the handling of the dough), cover with a large, upturned bowl and leave for 30 minutes.

Flour a bread-proving basket or line a bowl with a flour-covered tea towel. Gather up the dough, pulling the corners into the middle to make a tight ball, with the air all trapped inside. Carefully lift, seam-side up, into the basket or bowl and refrigerate overnight.

The next morning, preheat the oven to 220°C fan (475°F/gas 9) for 30 minutes with a lidded casserole dish inside. Cut a piece of baking parchment larger than the diameter of the basket or bowl.

Remove the dough from the fridge and turn it out onto the prepared baking parchment. Quickly and carefully remove the casserole from the oven. Slash the top of the sourdough with a small blade or sharp knife, then very carefully use the parchment to transfer the dough into the casserole. Pop the lid on, then bake for 25 minutes.

Remove the lid, then cook for a further 20 minutes, or until the loaf is perfectly golden. Carefully remove the dough from the dish using a spatula and leave to cool on a wire rack.

Seeded light rye loaf

MAKES **1 MEDIUM LOAF**

PREPARATION TIME **15 MINUTES, PLUS 2½ HOURS PROVING**

COOKING TIME **30 MINUTES**

This loaf has a slightly sweet, malty nuttiness to it and toasts amazingly. It's a great one to have in your repertoire.

250g (9oz) rye wholemeal flour, plus extra for dusting
250g (9oz) strong bread flour, plus extra for dusting
7g (¼oz) sachet of fast-action yeast
1 tsp flaky sea salt
300–320ml (10–11fl oz) warm water
1 tbsp honey
50g (2oz) mixed seeds
a little oil, for greasing

Put the rye flour and bread flour in a large bowl (or the bowl of a stand mixer). Put the yeast on one side of the bowl and the salt on the other. Mix 300ml (10fl oz) warm water with the honey, and stir it into the flour mixture using a wooden spoon. Add the extra water if it seems a little dry (all flours will vary slightly).

Knead on a lightly floured surface until the dough has come together and become slightly elastic – it won't be as smooth as a white dough because rye has less gluten. (Alternatively, you can use the dough hook in a stand mixer for about 6–8 minutes.) Put into an oiled bowl, cover with clingfilm (plastic wrap) and leave somewhere warm for 1½ hours, or until doubled in size.

Knock the air out of the dough on a lightly floured surface, then continue to knead to incorporate the seeds. Line a baking sheet with baking parchment. Shape the dough into an oval and place onto the prepared sheet. Cover with lightly oiled clingfilm (plastic wrap) and leave to rise for another hour. Alternatively, place into an oval or round flour-dusted proving basket and prove overnight in the fridge.

Preheat the oven to 200°C fan (450°F/gas 8).

Dust the top of the loaf with a little extra rye flour, and cut a couple of slashes in the top with a sharp knife. If you have used a proving basket, preheat a baking tray in the oven and turn the loaf out onto it. Bake for 25–30 minutes until risen and golden, and hollow-sounding if tapped underneath. Cool on a wire rack.

Butters, Dips & Spreads

Homemade butter

MAKES **250–280G (9–10oz)**

PREPARATION TIME **10 MINUTES**

Making your own butter is so simple – and is far superior to the store-bought stuff. The bonus, as well, is the leftover buttermilk

500ml (17fl oz) double cream
flaky sea salt (optional)

Put the double cream into a free-standing mixer (with the plastic guard on if possible!) and begin to whisk slowly before increasing the speed. The cream will go from a soft whip to a stiff peak, and then beyond, to split – and become butter (which will stick to the balloon whisk) and buttermilk. Put the butter solids into a muslin and squeeze out any excess liquid. Season with flaky sea salt if using as straight butter, then wrap in baking parchment.

Chill for up to 1 week in the fridge, or freeze for up to 2 months.

Anchovy butter

MAKES **ABOUT 150G (5oz)**

PREPARATION TIME **5 MINUTES**

This is a nod to the Italian *pane, acciughe e burro* – bread, anchovy and butter. I've amalgamated the butter and anchovy to make sure it all melts into hot toasted bread, and I like to make it with my own Homemade butter (left). Top with extra anchovies or a poached egg, if you like.

125g (4oz) unsalted butter at room temperature
7 anchovy fillets in olive oil, drained and roughly chopped
½ tsp flaky sea salt

Put all the ingredients in a food processor and blitz to combine. Serve on hot toasted brown sourdough.

Tip You can save any buttermilk (the liquid) to use in my Date and caraway soda bread (page 16).

Miso butter

MAKES **ABOUT 150G (5oz)**

PREPARATION TIME **5 MINUTES**

This two-ingredient miso butter is an easy way to add some umami to your buttered toast failsafe. Of course, it is perfect made with Homemade butter (opposite).

125g (4oz) unsalted butter at room temperature
2 tbsp white miso paste

Put the butter and miso paste into a food processor and pulse until smooth.

Pea and ricotta dip

SERVES **4–6**

PREPARATION TIME **5 MINUTES**

Pea and mint are the most fantastic combination – they taste like the smell of a summer garden. Here, the ricotta smooths out both their flavours, with a little tang from the pecorino and lemon juice. It's perfect for a garden party, along with some other dips and a big basket of toasted breads.

200g (7oz) frozen peas, defrosted in boiled water
250g (9oz) ricotta, drained
1½ tbsp mint, leaves roughly chopped, plus extra leaves to serve
1 lemon, zest and juice
20g pecorino, grated
flaky sea salt and freshly ground black pepper
extra virgin olive oil
toasted pitta chips or griddled toast
extra mint leaves

Put all the ingredients into a food processor with some salt and lots of freshly ground pepper. Mix until blended. Serve with toasted pitta chips for dipping, or spooned onto big sheets of griddled toast, drizzled with extra virgin olive oil and scattered with extra mint leaves.

Maple bacon butter

MAKES **ABOUT 125G (4oz)**

PREPARATION TIME **5 MINUTES**

This butter has little pops of sweet saltiness and is a great variation to regular butter. Try making it with Homemade butter (page 26) and serving it in place of your normal spread on toast with scrambled egg, on hot scones, or with beans on toast!

4 slices of smoked bacon
1 tbsp maple syrup
½ tsp flaky sea salt
125g (4oz) unsalted butter, at room temperature and roughly chopped

Put the bacon in a large non-stick frying pan. Top with a sheet of baking parchment and then another frying pan or large saucepan – making sure it is pushing down on the bacon to ensure it gets nice and crispy! Cook for 10 minutes over a medium heat, then carefully turn and cook for another 5 minutes. Remove to some kitchen paper to cool.

Finely chop the bacon, then put in a food processor bowl with the maple syrup, salt and butter. Blitz together until smooth – adding a little more salt to taste, if you like. Serve with ... toast! It's delicious on hot toasted cinnamon bagels, too.

Mackerel pâté

SERVES **4**

PREPARATION TIME **5 MINUTES**

Mackerel pâté is a Christmas staple in my house – the perfect in-between meal. It makes a fantastic sharing dish or a great light lunch. When I went to Belize in 2019, I was amazed to find them serving it in beach cafés, with stacks of tortilla chips and a bottle of hot sauce on the side – a wonderful addition.

2 smoked mackerel fillets (about 180g/6½oz each), skin discarded
100g (3½oz) cottage cheese
75g (2½oz) cream cheese
juice of 1 lemon, plus extra, to taste
sea salt and freshly ground black pepper
brown sourdough or rye bread, to toast
hot sauce (optional)

Combine all the ingredients in a food processor with plenty of pepper and a good sprinkle of sea salt. Blitz, then check for seasoning/lemony-ness. Add more to taste. Serve with a pile of toast!

Salmon terrine

SERVES **8**

PREPARATION TIME **15 MINUTES, PLUS 4 HOURS CHILLING**

This makes a wonderfully rich terrine – the cream cheese countered with a little zing from the crème fraîche and the saltiness of the capers. It is a great sharing starter, but equally delicious if you omit the smoked salmon on the outside and just blitz it together to make a smoked salmon mousse. Leftovers piled into toasted bagels get 10/10 in my book.

300g (10½oz) smoked salmon slices
150g (5oz) roast salmon slices
100g (3½oz) smoked salmon trimmings (or roughly chopped smoked salmon)
280g (10oz) cream cheese
100g (3½oz) lighter crème fraîche
1 tbsp horseradish
zest and juice of 1 lemon
2 tbsp capers, drained and roughly chopped
1½ tbsp chopped dill fronds
sea salt and freshly ground black pepper
sunflower oil, for greasing
mini cornichons
Melba toast or toasted sourdough

Use sunflower oil to lightly grease a 900g (2lb) loaf tin, then double line with clingfilm (plastic wrap).

Use the smoked salmon slices to line the tin, leaving an overhang (or some leftover to cover the top of the terrine).

Put the roast salmon slices and salmon trimmings in a food processor and pulse until roughly chopped. Add the cream cheese and crème fraîche and blend to combine. Then add the horseradish, lemon zest and juice, capers and dill. Season with salt and a generous amount of black pepper, then pulse to combine.

Spoon into the loaf tin, then fold any smoked salmon over the top (or cover with more smoked salmon). Cover the top with clingfilm (plastic wrap) and refrigerate for at least 4 hours.

Slice and serve with cornichons and Melba toast or toasted sourdough.

Flavoured schmears

EACH RECIPE SERVES **4**

PREPARATION TIME **15 MINUTES**

Just mix to combine – it couldn't be easier. With Yiddish origins, 'schmear' often refers to the cream you would put on a bagel – and these would all be excellent accompaniments to some smoked salmon or pastrami. They're a good selection to have up your sleeve if you're doing a 'build-your-own' breakfast buffet.

'EVERYTHING BAGEL' SCHMEAR
200g (7oz) cream cheese
2 tsp black sesame seeds
1½ tsp garlic granules
1½ tsp onion granules
2 tsp poppy seeds
2 tsp toasted sesame seeds
large pinch of flaky sea salt

FOR THE SPRING ONION SCHMEARS
200g (7oz) cream cheese
2–3 spring onions, finely chopped

FOR THE CAPER SCHMEARS
200g (7oz) cream cheese
2 tbsp capers, drained and roughly chopped

4 bagels

Mix together the ingredients for your chosen filling. Slice your bagels in half and toast lightly. Spread with your filling and sandwich together or leave open.

Whipped feta

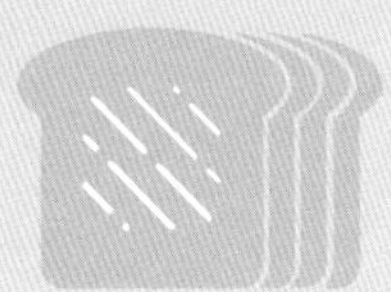

SERVES **4**

PREPARATION TIME **5 MINUTES**

This dip couldn't be more straightforward. Salty and simple, I've seasoned using parsley, but it's great for using up the tail-end of any herbs you've got in the fridge – dill, basil, coriander – they all taste great.

250g (9oz) feta
2 tbsp extra virgin olive oil
1 garlic clove, crushed
135g (4½oz) natural yogurt
1½ tbsp roughly chopped parsley
flaky sea salt and freshly ground black pepper
toasted flatbreads or pitta
a selection of other dips

Put the feta into a food processor and blitz until it's all broken down. Add the remaining ingredients plus some sea salt, if liked, and freshly ground black pepper. Blitz again until smooth.

Serve with a mezze of other dips and toasted flatbreads or pitta.

Hummus

SERVES **4**

PREPARATION TIME **10 MINUTES**

COOKING TIME **5 MINUTES**

I could happily eat hummus all day, every day. I used to intentionally burn white sliced bread in the toaster so I could get that umami flavour coming through, but now I prefer serving my hummus with a lightly golden flatbread and an array of other dips. I've tried and tested this recipe many times over the years and think I've finally honed my perfect hummus - silky smooth with the right balance of heat and freshness from the garlic and lemon.

400g (14oz) can of chickpeas
¼ tsp bicarbonate of soda
1 large (or 2 small) garlic cloves, crushed
80ml (3fl oz) tahini
juice of 1 lemon
½ tsp ground cumin
2 tbsp extra virgin olive oil, plus extra to serve
1 tsp za'atar
flaky sea salt and freshly ground black pepper
toasted pitta or flatbreads, to serve

Put the chickpeas and their liquid in a saucepan with the bicarbonate of soda. Simmer for 5 minutes, then leave to sit and cool slightly for another 10 minutes.

Tip into a food processor with the garlic, tahini, lemon juice, olive oil and ground cumin, and blitz until smooth. Season to taste with salt and pepper. Spoon into a serving bowl, drizzle with extra oil and sprinkle with za'atar. Serve with toasted pitta or flatbreads.

Babaganoush

SERVES **4**

PREPARATION TIME **5 MINUTES, PLUS DRAINING**

COOKING TIME **1 HOUR**

This wonderful Levantine starter is a staple in any mezze spread. Here, I've given it its iconic smokiness by grilling the aubergine, but you could cook it over the open flames of a gas hob, or even chuck it into the embers of a barbecue.

2 medium aubergines
2 tbsp olive oil
3 tbsp tahini
2 tbsp lemon juice
2 garlic cloves, crushed
1 tbsp chopped parsley leaves
flaky sea salt and freshly ground black pepper
pomegranate seeds
toasted flatbreads

Preheat the grill to high. Prick the aubergines with a fork, then grill for 50–60 minutes, turning regularly until the skins are really blackened and crumpling like charred paper. Leave to cool completely.

Peel and discard the aubergine skin. Set the flesh in a colander over a bowl to get rid of any bitter juices for 5–10 minutes. Roughly chop the aubergine, then turn into a bowl. Add the olive oil, tahini, lemon juice, garlic and parsley. Season to taste with salt and pepper, then mix to combine. Spoon into a bowl and scatter with pomegranate seeds. Serve with toasted flatbreads.

Taramasalata

SERVES **4**

PREPARATION TIME **15 MINUTES**

This Greek dip is made from cod roe (*tarama*) and is rich, smoky and moreish. The garnish of a single black olive reminds me of a holiday in Crete, this solitary punctuation mark signalling the beginning of a feast.

100g (3½oz) crustless stale white bread, roughly cubed and soaked in water for 5 minutes
250g (9oz) smoked cod roe
1 garlic clove, crushed
75ml (2½fl oz) rapeseed oil
125ml (4fl oz) olive oil, plus extra to drizzle
juice of 1 lemon
flaky sea salt and freshly ground black pepper
1 pitted black olive
toasted pitta or flatbread, to serve

Squeeze as much water out of the bread as possible and put the bread into the bowl of a food processor. Peel the thicker outer skin away from the cod roe, and spoon the eggs into the food processor with the crushed garlic. Start to run the food processor. Combine the oils in a small jug and slowly add the oil to the food processor to make a smooth mixture. Season with salt and pepper to taste, add the lemon juice, then blitz again to combine. Add extra lemon juice, to taste. Top with an extra drizzle of olive oil and a single black olive, and serve with toasted pitta or flatbread.

Chicken liver pâté

SERVES **6–8**

PREPARATION TIME **15 MINUTES**

COOKING TIME **20 MINUTES**

A lot of people have a love/hate relationship with pâté. Offal is divisive, the flavours are sometimes thought too rich, and the brandy and mustard give it strong undertones. But this recipe is a fine balance of all those elements – resulting in something deliciously rich with a hint of sweetness – perfect for a plate of Melba toast or a stack of warm sourdough, the buttery crust melting on top.

1 tbsp sunflower oil
I red onion, finely chopped
3 garlic cloves, crushed
180g (6½oz) salted butter plus 75g (2½oz) melted butter, to top
400g (14oz) chicken livers, any tough or sinewy bits trimmed
5 sprigs of thyme, leaves picked, plus extra leaves to finish
2 tbsp brandy
2 tsp Dijon mustard
flaky sea salt and freshly ground black pepper
Melba toast or toasted brown sourdough, to serve

Heat a large, heavy-based non-stick pan over a medium heat. Add the sunflower oil, then the onion and cook for 10–12 minutes until softened. Add the garlic and cook for another minute until fragrant. Remove the onions and garlic to a food processor and return the pan to the hob. Add 20g (¾oz) of the butter and the livers. Season with salt and pepper, and cook over a medium heat until the livers are browned all over but still pink in the middle (about 2–3 minutes), then put in a sieve set over a bowl to remove any bitter juices.

Add the thyme to the pan and toast for 30 seconds until fragrant, then add the brandy. Warm the brandy, stirring, until the sauce has nearly taken up the brown bits from the base of the pan. Remove from the heat, then add the remaining 160g (5½oz) of butter to the pan to melt. Add this liquid, along with the livers and mustard, to the food processor. Season, then blitz to combine to a smooth mixture. Spoon into a wide-based bowl and smooth the top. Pour the remaining melted butter on top and scatter with some extra thyme leaves. Cool to room temperature, then cover with clingfilm (plastic wrap) and chill.

Green olive tapenade

SERVES **4**

PREPARATION TIME **5 MINUTES**

The green olives and lemon zest in this recipe make this tapenade wonderfully light and zingy - perfect on crostini, as is, or topped with lemony chicken or thinly sliced steak!

200g (7oz) pitted green olives
1 tbsp chopped parsley leaves
3–5 anchovies (depending how salty you like it)
25g (¾oz) capers, drained
2 tbsp extra virgin olive oil
zest and juice of 1 lemon
toasted ciabatta, to serve

Put all the ingredients into a food processor and pulse until it forms a coarse paste. Serve with thinly sliced ciabatta toast (crostini). It goes beautifully with a glass of fizz, if you like.

Seasoned labneh balls

SERVES **6–8**

PREPARATION TIME **10 MINUTES, PLUS STRAINING OVERNIGHT**

This Middle Eastern strained yogurt is rich but simple! By rolling the mixture into individual balls, you can flavour it with whatever you fancy – ready and prepped to spread onto warm toasted bread.

1kg (2lb 4oz) 5% Greek yogurt
1 tsp flaky sea salt
35g (1oz) za'atar or 28g (scant 1oz) chilli flakes
flaky sea salt
toasted pitta or flatbread
a drizzle of honey (optional)

Combine the yogurt and salt in a bowl, then spoon into a bowl lined with muslin. Tie the muslin tightly round the yogurt, placing a wooden spoon through the knot in the middle. Use the wooden spoon to suspend the muslin over a deep bowl or stock pot. Refrigerate overnight or for up to 24 hours. Give the muslin a final squeeze to make sure you've strained off any liquid. Empty the labneh into a bowl.

Put the za'atar or chilli flakes in a shallow bowl. Take 1 tablespoon of labneh and roll into a ball, which you then roll through the za'atar or chilli flakes. Serve mashed onto toasted pitta or flatbread, with a sprinkle of flaky sea salt; on the chilli labneh you can also add a drizzle of honey, if liked.

Tip Only flavour half the labneh mix and use the remainer for Roasted squash with labneh and tarragon agrodolce (page 136).

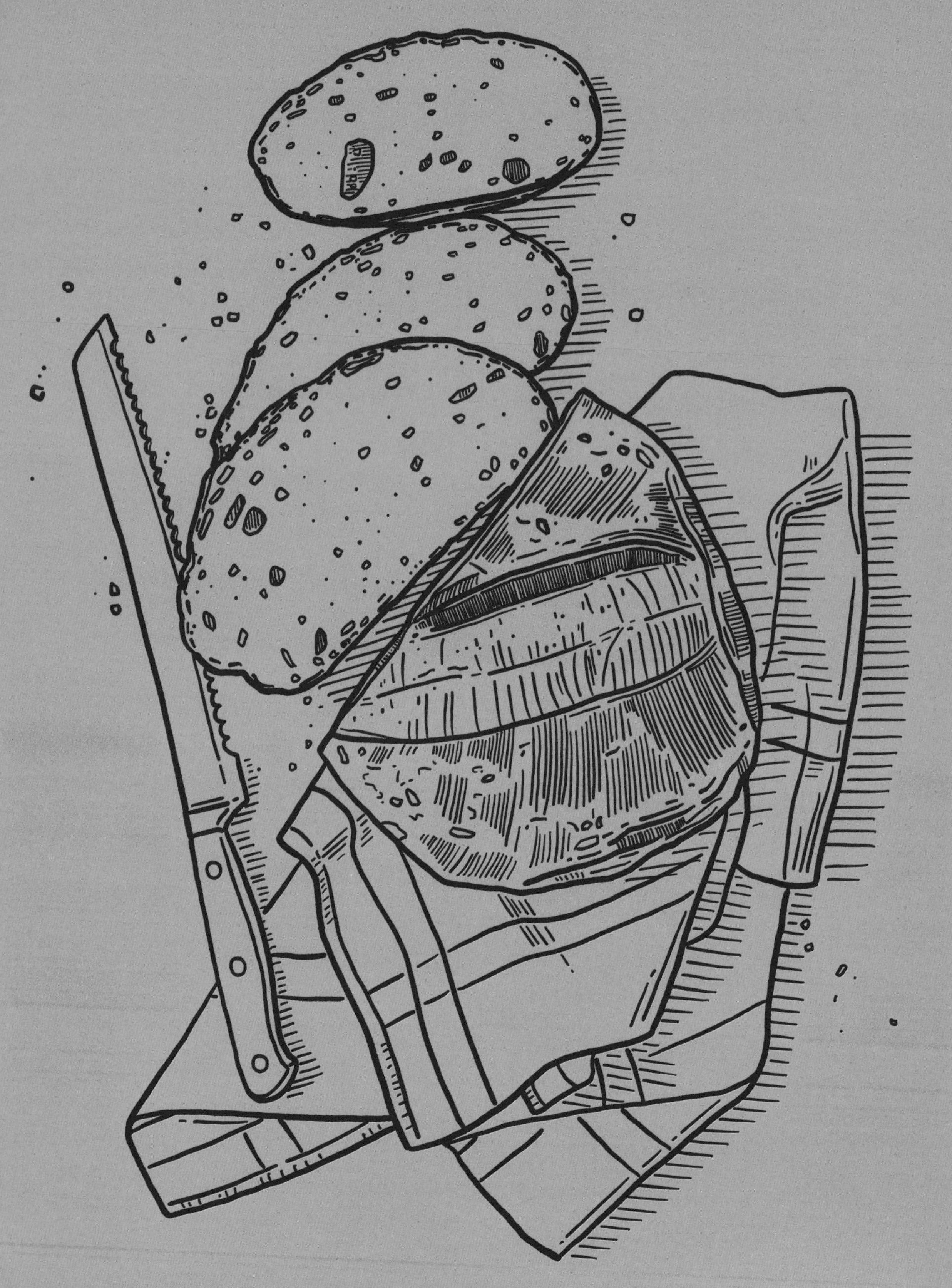

Small & Light Bites

Romesco sauce with charred tenderstem

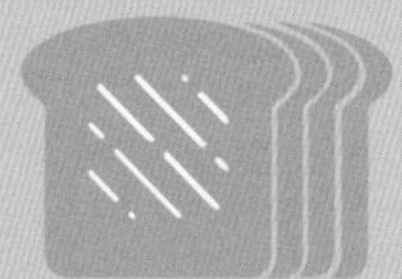

SERVES **4**

PREPARATION TIME **5 MINUTES**

COOKING TIME **10 MINUTES**

I absolutely love romesco sauce – the smoky sweetness of the peppers and paprika, countered by the acidity of the vinegar, and the heat of the garlic. I've topped this with tenderstem, but it would be delicious with a piece of fish – after all, it was inspired by the fishermen of Catalonia.

100g (3½oz) blanched almonds
3 tbsp extra virgin olive oil
200g (7oz) roasted red peppers (drained weight)
2 garlic cloves, crushed
2 tbsp tomato purée
1 tsp smoked paprika
2 tbsp sherry vinegar
1 tbsp chopped parsley leaves, plus extra to serve
150g (5oz) tenderstem broccoli, trimmed and halved
4 slices of sourdough
flaky sea salt and freshly ground black pepper

Place a frying pan over a medium-high heat. Add the almonds with ½ tablespoon of the olive oil and fry for 4–5 minutes until golden, stirring often to ensure they don't burn. Tip into a high-speed blender with 2 more tablespoons of olive oil, the peppers, garlic, tomato purée, paprika and sherry vinegar. Season with salt and pepper, then blitz until smooth before stirring through the chopped parsley.

Toss the broccoli in the remaining ½ tablespoon of olive oil. Return the frying pan to the hob and put over a high heat. Add the broccoli and cook for 3–4 minutes, turning until charred. Toast the sourdough, then top with the romeseco sauce and the charred broccoli, finishing with a final scattering of parsley.

Shell-on prawns and aioli

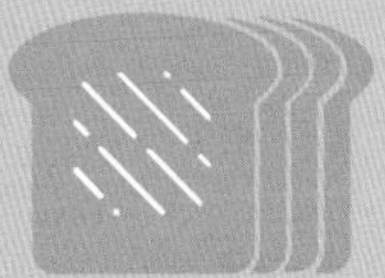

SERVES **2**

PREPARATION TIME **10 MINUTES**

COOKING TIME **5 MINUTES**

Another recipe that relies on simple and delicious ingredients, this easy aioli is an amazing toast-topper to have up your sleeve. The griddled prawns are ready in less than 10 minutes and make a meal that will transport you to a Mediterranean coast.

2 egg yolks
½ tbsp Dijon mustard
4 garlic cloves, crushed
150ml (5fl oz) olive oil
juice of ½ lemon, rest cut into wedges
flaky sea salt and freshly ground black pepper
4 pieces of toasted sourdough
8 shell-on tiger prawns

Combine the egg yolks, mustard and garlic in the small bowl of a food processor. With the engine running, very slowly, add the olive oil in a steady trickle. Season with salt and pepper to taste, and add the lemon juice before checking the flavour and adjusting to suit.

Set a griddle over a medium-high heat. Griddle the sourdough, then set aside. Add the prawns to the griddle and cook for about 2 minutes on each side until the shells are bright red/orange and slightly charred.

Serve the prawns with the aioli and toasted sourdough.

Coronation eggs on toast

SERVES **4**

PREPARATION TIME **10 MINUTES**

COOKING TIME **20 MINUTES**

With all the flavours of coronation chicken, you really don't miss the meat here. It's a fun twist on an egg sandwich and is super moreish.

2 tbsp white wine vinegar
1 tbsp caster sugar
1 celery stick, sliced
30g (1oz) sultanas or raisins
6 medium eggs
1 tbsp sunflower oil
3 banana shallots, thinly sliced
1 tbsp medium curry powder
1 tsp ground cumin
2 tbsp flaked almonds
60g (2¼oz) mayonnaise
40g (1½oz) natural yogurt
juice of ½ lemon
flaky sea salt and freshly ground black pepper
2 garlic and coriander naans
3 tbsp mango chutney

Put the vinegar in a small saucepan with the caster sugar and 50ml (2fl oz) water. Bring to a simmer. Put the celery and raisins in a small heatproof bowl and pour the warm vinegar mixture over the top. Set aside to pickle while you prepare the rest.

Bring a pan of water to the boil. Add the eggs and cook for 9 minutes, then run under cold water before putting into a bowl of cold (iced, if possible) water to cool completely.

Meanwhile, heat the sunflower oil in a frying pan. Add the sliced shallots and cook for 8–10 minutes until softened. Add the curry powder and ground cumin, and cook for another minute until fragrant. Remove to a bowl. Return the frying pan to the heat and add the almonds. Cook for 8–10 minutes until toasted (alternatively use pre-toasted almond slices, but they're never quite as tasty).

When the eggs are cool enough, peel off the shells. Add half the eggs to the bowl with the shallots and mash with the back of a fork. Add the mayonnaise, yogurt and lemon juice. Season with salt and pepper and mix to combine. Finely chop the remaining eggs and stir them through too (for a little more texture).

Drain the pickled celery and raisins and stir half through the egg mixture.

Toast the naan breads. Spread each with some mango chutney and top with the egg mixture. Scatter with the remaining celery and raisins, and finish with the toasted almonds. Cut each naan in half to serve.

Chickpea and anchovy toasts

SERVES **2**

PREPARATION TIME **5 MINUTES**

COOKING TIME **10 MINUTES**

This is such a great 10-minute meal, easily halved or doubled, depending on hunger and guests. The anchovies completely melt away to make an umami emulsification, with the salty pops of capers. You could leave out the cream, but I find that it makes the whole dish come together. It works perfectly well with ordinary chickpeas if you can't get hold of queen ones.

2 tbsp extra virgin olive oil, plus extra to serve
3 garlic cloves, sliced
8 anchovy filets in olive oil
200g (7oz) queen chickpeas (drained weight)
¼ tsp chilli flakes
2 tbsp capers, drained
juice of ½ lemon
2 tbsp double cream
flaky sea salt and freshly ground black pepper
2 slices of light rye or brown sourdough
1½ tbsp roughly chopped parsley

Heat the olive oil in a medium non-stick frying pan over a medium-high heat. Add the garlic and anchovies and cook for 5–6 minutes, stirring, until the anchovies have broken down, the garlic is turning golden and the oil is foaming. Add the chickpeas, followed by the chilli flakes and capers. Sizzle and cook through for a minute before adding the lemon juice. Cook for a minute, then remove from the heat and stir in the cream and parsley. Grind in a little salt, if liked, and plenty of black pepper.

Toast the bread, drizzle a little more extra virgin olive oil over it, then pile on the chickpeas and serve sprinkled with parsley.

Caesar garlic toast

SERVES **4**

PREPARATION TIME **10 MINUTES**

COOKING TIME **15 MINUTES**

This take on a Caesar salad is perfectly juicy and crunchy – the ciabatta becoming a giant croûton by pan-frying in aromatic homemade garlic oil. It's the perfect summer lunch.

FOR THE CAESAR DRESSING

10g (½oz) anchovies in oil, drained (plus optional extra to serve)
1 garlic clove, crushed
75g (2½oz) mayonnaise
1 tbsp white wine vinegar
1 tsp wholegrain mustard
1 tbsp water
freshly ground black pepper

FOR THE SALAD

1 large chicken breast
4 tbsp olive oil
juice of ½ lemon
2 garlic cloves, sliced

TO SERVE

1 half ciabatta, halved through the middle (the 'waist'), then halved again (to make 4 toasts)
1 little gem lettuce, shredded
10g (½oz) parmesan, grated, plus extra shavings

Put all the dressing ingredients into a high-speed blender with a good grind of black pepper. Mix to combine (otherwise mash the anchovies in a pestle and mortar and then combine with the remaining ingredients).

Butterfly the chicken breast and place in a bowl with 1 tablespoon of olive oil and the lemon juice. Season with salt and pepper. Preheat a wide-based non-stick frying pan to medium-high, add 1 tablespoon of olive oil, and then add the chicken. Fry for 3½ minutes on each side, or until the chicken is golden and the juices run clear. Set aside on a board to rest, then slice to serve. Carefully wipe out the pan.

Return the frying pan to the heat. Add the remaining oil and heat to medium. Add the garlic and heat until the garlic is turning golden and fragrant. Carefully remove. Add the ciabatta to the oil, cut-side down, and continue to fry until the bread is golden and toasted.

Put the shredded lettuce into a bowl with the grated parmesan. Add most of the Caesar dressing.

Top the toasted bread with the shredded lettuce, chicken slices, remaining dressing and parmesan shavings (and crunchy fried garlic, if liked). Add extra anchovies, if using.

Soy-marinated eggs with creamy kimchi

SERVES **4**

PREPARATION TIME **10 MINUTES, PLUS MARINADING**

COOKING TIME **15 MINUTES**

I've suggested serving this on Japanese milk bread (*Hokkaido*), which is light and fluffy (like clouds) and the perfect base for the light pepperiness of the kimchi-flavoured cream cheese. If you can't find it, it is easily exchangeable for some soft white bread! The soy-marinated eggs absorb all the essence of its salty and citrussy surrounds – and they look great, too!

4 eggs
120ml (4fl oz) light soy sauce
3 garlic cloves, sliced
1 chilli, deseeded and sliced
2 tbsp mirin
2 tbsp rice or white wine vinegar (or black vinegar, if possible)
220ml (7½fl oz) water
150g (5oz) kimchi, finely chopped, plus 20g (¾oz) for serving
100g (3½oz) cream cheese
4 pieces of milk bread, or milk bread buns, toasted
½ tbsp toasted sesame seeds
2 spring onions, finely sliced

Bring a pan of water to the boil. Carefully lower in the eggs and cook for 7 minutes. Remove with a slotted spoon to a bowl of iced water and leave to cool while you prepare the marinade.

Put the soy sauce, garlic, chilli, mirin and vinegar in a saucepan with the water. Bring to the boil then simmer for 5 minutes. Peel the eggs and put into a small, heatproof bowl. Pour the marinade over the top. Marinate for at least an hour (or overnight if you have time). Refrigerate when cooled (if marinating for more than an hour). Drain before serving.

Combine the kimchi and cream cheese in a bowl. Spread onto the toasted bread. Top with extra kimchi and a halved egg per serving. Scatter with the sesame seeds and spring onion.

Griddled sardines

SERVES **4**

PREPARATION TIME **5 MINUTES**

COOKING TIME **10 MINUTES**

The smell of sardines cooking on a griddle (or preferably over coal) immediately transports me to Portugal and Spain. This recipe is so simple, but the components all play their part – a really good olive oil is crucial here.

juice of 1 lemon, plus extra wedges to serve
2 tbsp extra virgin olive oil, plus extra to finish
8 sardines, gutted and cleaned
4 slices of sourdough
2 garlic cloves, sliced through the middle
1 tbsp finely chopped parsley
flaky sea salt and freshly ground black pepper

Combine the lemon juice and olive oil and season, then rub on the inside and outside of the sardine fillets. Preheat a griddle pan to high and cook the fillets for 2 minutes on each side. Toast the bread and then rub with the cut garlic cloves. Top the toast with the sardines and drizzle with oil, then scatter with parsley and salt flakes. Garnish with lemon wedges. To eat – flake the meat off the sardines, discarding the head, skeleton and tail, which will all come away easily.

Caponata

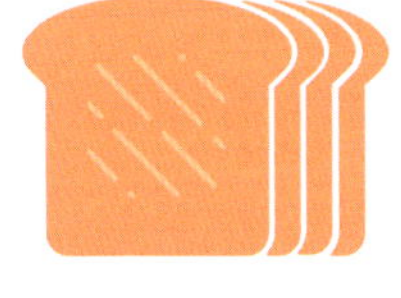

SERVES **4 (1 X CIABATTA)**

PREP **10 MINUTES**

COOKING TIME **45 MINUTES**

This Sicilian aubergine stew is amazing served hot or at room temperature. There is a lot of debate over the right way to cook and garnish it, so I think that leaves it all open to interpretation. I've served mine on toasted ciabatta, but you could also serve it as part of a selection of dips if you fancied.

2½ tbsp olive oil, plus extra for drizzling
2 aubergines, cut into rough 2cm (¾in) dice
2 celery sticks, halved lengthways then sliced
1 red onion, sliced
4 vine tomatoes, roughly chopped
50ml red wine vinegar
1 tsp caster sugar
½ tsp chilli flakes
200ml (7fl oz) passata
50g (2oz) green olives, sliced
50g (2oz) capers, drained
60g (2¼oz) raisins
flaky sea salt
1 ciabatta, sliced through the middle then halved again
2 tsp toasted flaked almonds
1 tbsp roughly chopped parsley

Preheat 1 tablespoon of olive oil in a large frying pan over a medium-high heat. Add half the aubergine and fry for 4–5 minutes until browned on all sides. Remove to a plate. Repeat with another 1 tablespoon of olive oil and the remaining aubergine. Reduce the heat to medium. Add a final ½ tablespoon of olive oil to the pan and then the celery and onion. Season with salt, then fry for 15 minutes. Add the tomatoes and cook for another 5 minutes until starting to mush down. Add the vinegar, sugar, chilli flakes, passata, olives, capers and raisins, and return the aubergine to the pan. Put the lid on and simmer for 20 minutes. Leave to cool to room temperature.

Toast the ciabatta quarters and drizzle with olive oil, then pile with the caponata. Finish with a scattering of almonds and chopped parsley.

Charred pointed cabbage with miso mashed butterbeans

SERVES **4**

PREPARATION TIME **5 MINUTES**

COOKING TIME **35 MINUTES**

The indulgent miso butterbeans make such a comforting base to the umami cabbage. The flavours would hold up to a brown or wholemeal sourdough, but it's an easy one to mix and match.

1 pointed cabbage, cut into 6 lengthways
2 tbsp olive oil
2 tbsp sesame oil
1 tbsp honey
1 tbsp rice vinegar
1 tbsp light soy sauce
1 red chilli, deseeded and finely chopped
1 tbsp salted butter
2 garlic cloves, crushed
3 tbsp miso
400g (14oz) butterbeans (drained weight)
juice of ½ lemon
flaky sea salt and freshly ground black pepper
4 slices of wholemeal sourdough

Toss the cabbage in 1 tablespoon of olive oil in a bowl and season with salt and pepper. Preheat a griddle pan to high. Add the cabbage and cook for 6 minutes on each of the flat sides.

Meanwhile, preheat the oven to 200°C fan (450°F/gas 8) and line a baking sheet with baking parchment.

Combine the sesame oil, honey, rice vinegar, soy sauce and chopped chilli in a small bowl. When the cabbage is charred, transfer to the prepared baking sheet and brush with the dressing. Put in the oven to cook for 8 minutes, then turn each piece of cabbage, baste, and scatter with the sesame seeds. Cook for another 8–10 minutes while you prepare the mash.

Heat a frying pan over a medium heat. Add the butter and remaining 1 tablespoon of olive oil. Add the crushed garlic and allow to cook for a minute until fragrant. Add the miso and butterbeans. Heat through, then coarsely mash with a potato masher. Season with salt, then stir through the lemon juice.

Griddle the toast. Spread with the mashed miso and top each with a wedge of cabbage. Slice the remaining cabbage wedges and divide between the toasts.

Kale and garlicky white beans

SERVES **4**

PREPARATION TIME **5 MINUTES**

COOKING TIME **15 MINUTES**

The butterbeans are the star of this show, so buying a jar (instead of a tin) is the way to ensure extra buttery flavour. Making a nutritious and balanced meal, this might just be your new answer to the classic beans on toast.

1 tbsp olive oil
1 onion, thinly sliced
3 garlic cloves, crushed
140g (4½oz) chopped kale
570g (1lb 4½oz) jar of butterbeans
60g (2¼oz) pecorino, grated, plus extra to serve
zest and juice of 1 lemon
flaky sea salt and freshly ground black pepper
4 slices of toasted sourdough
extra virgin olive oil

Preheat the olive oil in a wide frying pan over a medium heat. Add the onion and cook for 7–8 minutes until softened. Add the garlic and fry for a minute before adding the kale and butterbeans, with their water. Allow the kale to wilt before stirring through the pecorino, lemon zest and juice. Season with salt and pepper, then pile onto the sourdough toast, drizzling with some extra virgin olive oil and an extra sprinkle of pecorino.

Gochujang egg mayo

SERVES **4**

PREPARATION TIME **10 MINUTES**

COOKING TIME **15 MINUTES**

Gochujang is a lightly sweetened Korean red chilli paste. All pastes vary, so you might want to sample it as you go and adjust the quantities to your taste; I like to use authentic Korean paste because it's nice and spicy. Serving with milk buns means you get a crusty outside and a soft fluffy middle. You can buy crispy onions in tubs or fry your own.

6 medium eggs
40g (1½oz) mayonnaise
2 tbsp gochujang paste
1 tsp rice vinegar
3 spring onions, trimmed and finely sliced
2 milk buns, halved
crispy onions, to serve

Bring a saucepan of water to the boil. Add the eggs and cook for 8 minutes. Run the pan under cold water, then transfer the eggs to a bowl of cold water (iced if possible) to cool completely. Peel the eggs and set one aside.

Roughly mash the remaining eggs in a bowl before adding the mayonnaise, gochujang, rice vinegar and the spring onion whites. Combine. Put the milk bread under the grill to toast. Cut the final boiled egg into 4 lengthways. Top the toasted milk buns with the gochujang egg mayo and an egg quarter, sprinkle with the spring onion greens, and finish with crispy onion.

Hoisin mushrooms

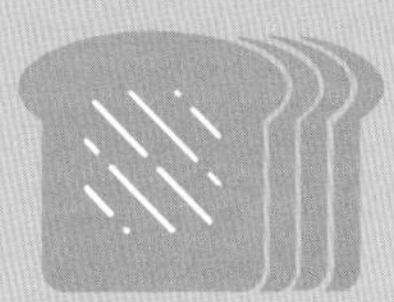

SERVES **2**

PREPARATION TIME **5 MINUTES**

COOKING TIME **10 MINUTES**

Mushrooms are the perfect vegetarian substitute to meat – and here they steal the show from traditional duck with all the accompaniments to Peking duck. By using vegan mayo, it's a great vegan feast, too.

2 spring onions, cut into 5cm (2in) lengths, then cut very thinly lengthways
1 tbsp sesame oil
250g (9oz) mushrooms, thinly sliced (I used a combination of shiitake and chestnut)
1 tsp Chinese five-spice
1 tbsp light soy sauce
2 tbsp hoisin sauce
2 slices of white bread
mayonnaise, to serve (vegan, if liked)
100g (3½oz) cucumber, deseeded and cut into matchsticks

Firstly, put the spring onion into iced water so the lengths can curl.

Place a wide-based frying pan over a high heat. Add the sesame oil, followed by the mushrooms. Cook for 8–10 minutes until all the moisture has cooked off and the mushrooms are looking brown and sticky. Add the Chinese five-spice and fry for 30 seconds before adding the soy sauce and removing from the heat. Stir through the hoisin sauce.

Toast your bread and spread with some mayo, then pile with the mushrooms. Drain the spring onions and sprinkle on top with the cucumber.

Crab and pickled cucumber on brioche

SERVES **2-4 (WITH LEFTOVER PICKED CUCUMBER)**

PREPARATION TIME **10 MINUTES, PLUS 10 MINUTES PICKLING**

I was inspired to create this recipe by the decadent and delicious Canadian idea of lobster served in brioche rolls. Such hedonism. The toasted brioche here accentuates the sweetness of the crab meat, and is also helped along by the kewpie mayo, which is made just from egg yolk and is nicely rich. The pickled cucumber adds a necessary salty acidity, with still some crunch - and the *togarashi* (seven spice) gives a little Japanese spice kick!

20g (¾oz) piece of ginger root, peeled and finely grated
80ml (3fl oz) rice vinegar
2 tbsp water
1 tbsp caster sugar
1 tsp flaky sea salt
½ cucumber, very thinly sliced (with a mandolin if possible)
200g (7oz) white crab meat
2 tbsp kewpie mayo, plus extra to serve
zest and juice of 1 lemon
4 slices of brioche
togarashi, to serve (optional)

Put the ginger, rice vinegar, water, caster sugar and salt into a wide jar and mix to dissolve the sugar. Add the cucumber and combine (gently shake with the lid on, if you can). Put in the fridge for 10 minutes.

Meanwhile, combine the crab meat with the kewpie mayo, lemon zest and juice. Toast the brioche.

Spread the brioche with a little extra kewpie, then top with the crab meat. Drain some of the sliced cucumber and use to top the crab, followed by a little dusting of *togarashi*.

Prawn toast

SERVES **4–6**

PREPARATION TIME **15 MINUTES**

COOKING TIME **15 MINUTES**

This Chinese takeaway classic is surprisingly easy to make, and it makes a pack of prawns go a long way! It's a great addition to a Chinese-inspired feast.

160g (5½oz) raw king prawns
1 spring onion, roughly chopped
15g (½oz) piece of ginger root, peeled and roughly chopped
2 garlic cloves, crushed
1 egg, beaten
1 tbsp cornflour
1 tbsp soy sauce
100g (3½oz) sesame seeds (you will have some spare)
5 slices of medium white bread, crusts removed
500ml (17fl oz) flavourless oil, such as groundnut, sunflower or vegetable
sweet chilli sauce, to serve

Blend the prawns, spring onion, ginger, garlic, egg, cornflour and soy sauce in a table mixer or food processor until it forms a smooth paste.

Put the sesame seeds into a shallow bowl. Cut the bread slices into 4 triangles and spread one side of each triangle with the prawn paste, then dip into the sesame seeds, pressing down gently.

Put the oil into a large, wide-based frying pan over a high heat until it reaches 180°C (350°F). Working in batches, fry the toasts for 1–2 minutes on each side until golden brown, then remove to a plate lined with kitchen paper. Serve with sweet chilli sauce for dipping.

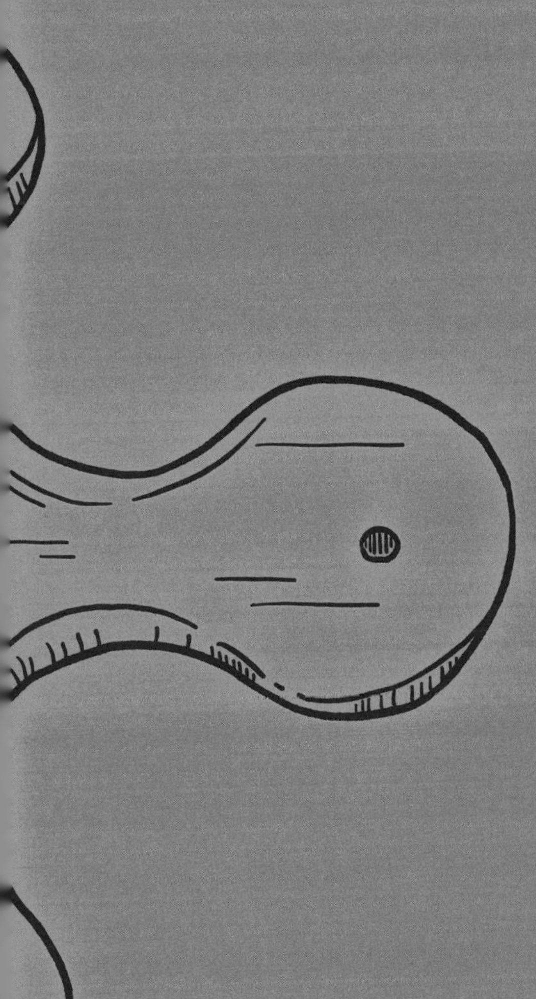

Breakfast & Brunch

Pan con tomate

SERVES **4–6**

PREPARATION TIME **15 MINUTES, PLUS 20 MINUTES TO DRAIN**

COOKING TIME **5 MINUTES**

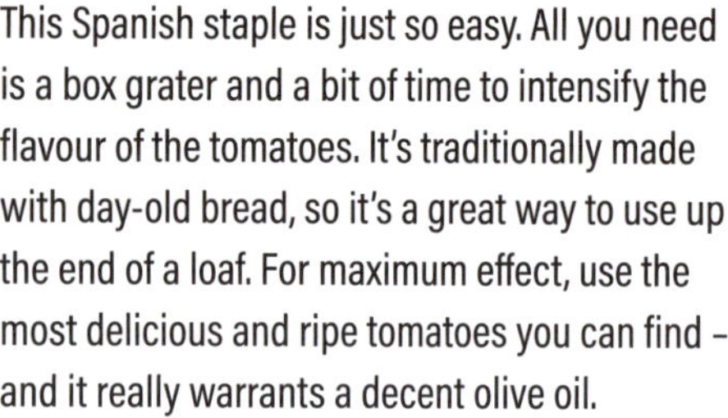

This Spanish staple is just so easy. All you need is a box grater and a bit of time to intensify the flavour of the tomatoes. It's traditionally made with day-old bread, so it's a great way to use up the end of a loaf. For maximum effect, use the most delicious and ripe tomatoes you can find – and it really warrants a decent olive oil.

6 ripe vine tomatoes (about 450g (1lb))
1 tsp flaky sea salt
4 slices of sourdough bread
1 fat garlic clove, skin on
extra virgin olive oil, to serve

Grate the tomatoes using a box grater, discarding the skins. Place the flesh in a sieve over a bowl, sprinkle with some salt and leave for 20 minutes to get rid of some of the excess water.

Toast the bread, cut the garlic in half (skin-on) and use to rub over the warm toasted bread. Top with the tomatoes and drizzle with oil.

Cheesy baked beans

SERVES **2**

PREPARATION TIME **10 MINUTES**

COOKING TIME **35 MINUTES**

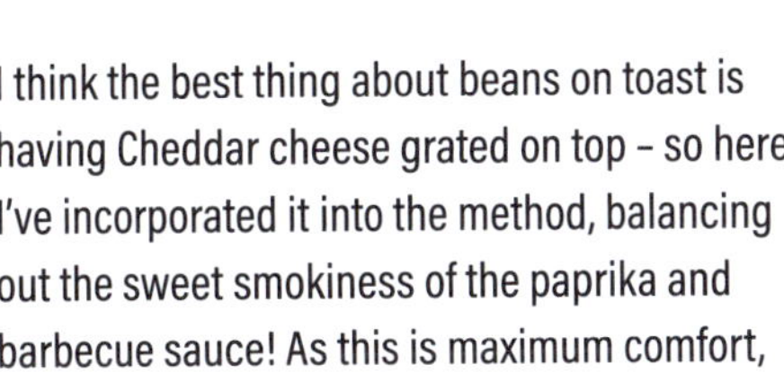

I think the best thing about beans on toast is having Cheddar cheese grated on top - so here I've incorporated it into the method, balancing out the sweet smokiness of the paprika and barbecue sauce! As this is maximum comfort, the toast is your choice.

1 tbsp olive oil
1 onion, chopped
2 garlic cloves, crushed
1 tsp smoked paprika
350ml (12¼fl oz) passata
1 tbsp cider vinegar
1 tbsp barbecue sauce
1 tbsp soft brown sugar
400g (14oz) can of cannellini beans, drained
50g Cheddar, grated
2 slices of bread, toasted and buttered

Heat the olive oil in a saucepan over a medium heat, then add the onions and cook for 6–8 minutes until softened. Add the garlic and fry for another minute. Add the paprika and fry for another few seconds until fragrant. Add the passata, vinegar, barbecue sauce, brown sugar and cannellini beans. Reduce to a simmer and cook for 20–25 minutes, uncovered, until the beans are softened and the sauce is thickened. Stir through the Cheddar. Serve on buttered toast!

Scandi-inspired salmon on rye

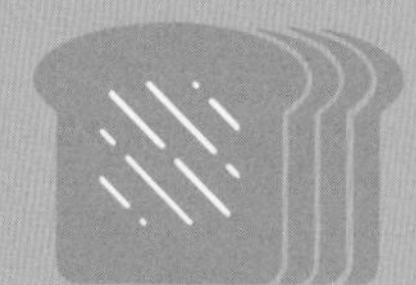

SERVES 4

PREPARATION TIME 5 MINUTES

COOKING TIME 10 MINUTES

This is my take on a Scandinavian open sandwich, a *smørrebrøt* – served as part of a *smörgåsbord* (buffet-style). Dill, salmon and some pickled onions – the perfect trio – all aboard a nutty, earthy rye toast.

3 tbsp white wine vinegar
1 tbsp water
1 tsp caster sugar
½ red onion, thinly sliced
1 tbsp chopped dill fronds, plus extra to serve
1 tbsp horseradish sauce
5 tbsp crème fraîche or soured cream
4 slices of rye bread
200g (7oz) smoked salmon slices
5 radishes, thinly sliced
flaky sea salt and freshly ground black pepper

Combine the white wine vinegar, water, caster sugar and a pinch of salt in a small saucepan and bring to a simmer. Put the onion in a heatproof bowl, then pour over the hot liquid and set aside for 10 minutes (or longer, if you have time).

Mix the chopped dill with the horseradish and crème fraîche or soured cream in a small bowl. Season with salt and pepper.

Toast the rye bread. Spread the dill cream over the rye bread and top with the salmon. Drain the pickled onions and scatter over the toast, along with the radishes and a final sprinkling of dill.

Black beans, corn, avocado and egg

SERVES **4**

PREPARATION TIME **10 MINUTES**

COOKING TIME **25 MINUTES**

The black beans themselves are enough of a reason to sample this toast – a slight nod to Mexican taco contents. The prep involves a bit of multi-tasking but is worth it for all the layers of flavours. This is the best way to brunch!

3 tbsp olive oil
1 onion, thinly sliced
2 garlic cloves, crushed
2 tbsp tomato purée
1 tsp sweet smoked paprika
1 tsp ground cumin
400g (14oz) can of black beans, drained
1 sprig of coriander, stalks chopped and leaves reserved
1 corn on the cob, kernels removed with a sharp knife
1 tbsp salted butter
4 eggs
4 large slices of seeded sourdough
1 large avocado, sliced
flaky sea salt and freshly ground black pepper
1 lime, cut into wedges
hot sauce (optional)

Preheat a wide-based frying pan over a medium heat. Add 1 tablespoon of the olive oil and then the onion. Cook for 8–10 minutes until softened.

Add the garlic, tomato purée, paprika and ground cumin and fry for 1 minute before adding the black beans with 150ml (5fl oz) water. Simmer for 10–12 minutes until the beans have softened and started to mush down. You can mash with the back of a wooden spoon to help it along a bit. Stir through the coriander stalks.

Meanwhile, heat another tablespoon of olive oil in a medium non-stick frying pan over a high heat. Add the corn and fry for 2–3 minutes until dark golden. Add the butter and remove from the heat, then transfer to a bowl. Season with salt and pepper.

Wipe out the pan and return to a medium-high heat. Add the final tablespoon of olive oil, then, when hot, add the eggs and fry for 1½–2 minutes until the edges of the egg are crisped and the white is set.

Toast the bread and then load up with the beans. Top with a fried egg, followed by the corn and some sliced avocado. Finish with the coriander leaves and a wedge of lime, and some hot sauce, if using.

Bacon and chipotle avocado

SERVES **2**

PREPARATION TIME **5 MINUTES**

COOKING TIME **5 MINUTES**

The chipotle paste in this dish is inspired by Mexican *salsa macha* – and makes the smashed avocado slightly sweet, while having that smoky warmth of the chipotle paste. I've served it with granary bread for that lovely maltiness, but feel free to mix and match.

2 tbsp sunflower oil
1 dried chipotle chilli, finely chopped (deseeded, if liked)
1 large garlic clove, crushed
½ tbsp honey
1 tbsp salted peanuts
4 slices of streaky bacon
1 ripe avocado, roughly chopped
½ lemon
2 slices of granary bread
flaky sea salt

Heat 1 tablespoon of the sunflower oil in a medium frying pan over a medium heat. Add the chopped chipotle and garlic and fry for 1–1½ minutes until fragrant, then remove from the heat.

Add the honey and peanuts, mix to combine, then transfer to a pestle and mortar and add a good pinch of flaky sea salt. Grind the mixture to a paste.

Carefully wipe out the frying pan and add the remaining sunflower oil to the pan. Heat over a medium-high heat until hot, then add the bacon. Cook for 2–3 minutes on each side until crisp. Drain on some kitchen paper.

Add the avocado to the pestle and mortar and use a fork to crush it all together, squeezing in a little lemon juice, to taste. Toast the bread, then drizzle with a little of the bacon oil. Spread with the avocado, then top with the bacon to serve.

Garlic mushrooms

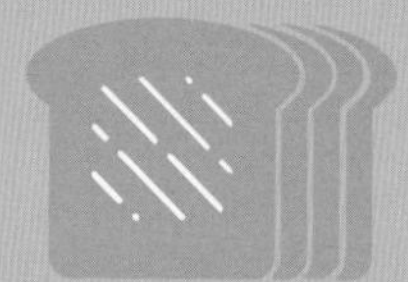

SERVES **2**

PREPARATION TIME **5 MINUTES**

COOKING TIME **10 MINUTES**

This is the kind of recipe that could even convert someone to loving mushrooms. Cooked down to a delicious texture, they are just a vessel for garlicky buttery perfection. A vegetarian staple.

1 tbsp olive oil
300g (10½oz) mushrooms, sliced (I used chestnut and portobello)
2 fat garlic cloves, crushed
50g (2oz) butter
1 tbsp chopped parsley
2 slices of sourdough
flaky sea salt and freshly ground black pepper

Heat the olive oil in a wide-based frying pan over a medium-high heat. Add the mushrooms and cook for 6–8 minutes, seasoning with some salt, until the water has evaporated out of the mushrooms and they are browned and sticky. Reduce the temperature and add the garlic. Fry for 30 seconds, stirring constantly. Remove from the heat. Add the butter, parsley and a good grind of black pepper. Serve on toasted sourdough – pouring all the garlicky butter over at the end.

Greens with pistachio pesto

SERVES **2**

PREPARATION TIME **10 MINUTES**

COOKING TIME **10 MINUTES**

This is a carb-lovers substitute for a green juice – for the times when you feel like you really need to load up on some veg, but just can't face a salad.

30 g (12oz) shelled pistachios
zest and juice of 1 lemon
2 small garlic cloves, crushed
30g (1oz) basil, leaves and stems roughly chopped
30g (1oz) parmesan, grated
3 tbsp extra virgin olive oil
3 tbsp water
½ tbsp olive oil
100g (3½oz) asparagus, woody tips trimmed and stalks halved
100g (3½oz) baby spinach leaves
100g (3½oz) frozen peas
2 slices of brown bread
flaky sea salt and freshly ground black pepper

To make the pesto sauce, start by toasting the pistachios for about 5 minutes in a medium non-stick frying pan over a medium heat until lightly fragrant. Remove to a bowl to cool, then transfer to a high-speed blender. Add the lemon zest and juice, garlic, basil, parmesan, extra virgin olive oil, water and seasoning. Blitz until smooth then taste – adding more garlic and lemon, to taste.

Return the pan to the heat and add the ½ tablespoon of olive oil, then add the asparagus and increase the heat. Fry for 1–1½ minutes before adding the spinach and peas with a splash of water, cooking over a high heat until the water has nearly evaporated and the spinach is wilted. Remove to a bowl with a slotted spoon and toss with half the pesto sauce.

Toast the bread, top with the remaining pesto, then top with all the veg and serve.

Creamy sausage and fennel

SERVES **2**

PREPARATION TIME **5 MINUTES**

COOKING TIME **15 MINUTES**

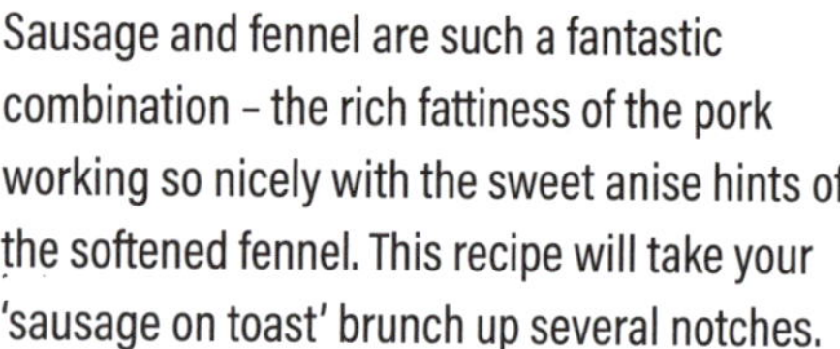

Sausage and fennel are such a fantastic combination – the rich fattiness of the pork working so nicely with the sweet anise hints of the softened fennel. This recipe will take your 'sausage on toast' brunch up several notches.

1½ tbsp olive oil
1 fennel bulb, thinly sliced, fronds reserved
3 Cumberland sausages
1 tsp fennel seeds
2 garlic cloves, crushed
125ml (4fl oz) chicken stock
50ml (2fl oz) single cream
25g (¾oz) parmesan, grated
juice of ½ lemon
2 large slices of sourdough
freshly ground black pepper
chilli flakes, to serve

Heat 1 tablespoon of the olive oil in a wide-based frying pan over a medium-high heat. Add the fennel and cook for 6–8 minutes until softened. Tip into a bowl.

Return the pan to the heat and add the remaining olive oil. Squeeze the sausage from its skin (if it has one) directly into the pan, breaking up with a wooden spoon to make little nuggets. Fry for about 2 minutes until browning.

Return the fennel to the pan with the fennel seeds and garlic and fry for another minute until fragrant. Add the stock and cook for 2 minutes until the stock is almost completely reduced. Turn down the heat and stir through the cream, parmesan and lemon juice to combine. Season with pepper.

Toast the sourdough and top with the sausage mixture, finishing with the fennel fronds and a sprinkle of chilli flakes.

Kippers and scrambled egg

SERVES **2**

PREPARATION TIME **5 MINUTES**

COOKING TIME **10 MINUTES**

This traditional British breakfast fish is quite an intense morning taste! The deeply smoked kippers are softened by the rich eggs and make a really sturdy start to the day.

30g (1oz) butter, plus extra to butter your toast
1 butterflied smoked kipper fillet
5 eggs
½ tsp curry powder (optional)
2 slices of sourdough
1½ tbsp roughly chopped parsley
1 lemon, cut into wedges
freshly ground black pepper

Melt half the butter in a medium frying pan over a medium-high heat. Add the butterflied kipper fillet and cook for 2–3 minutes on each side, until hot through.

Meanwhile, melt the remaining butter in a small saucepan over a medium heat. Whisk together the eggs and curry powder, if using, and season with pepper (the kippers will be very salty). Add to the saucepan and cook, stirring constantly, for about 3–3½ minutes until silky smooth but cooked through.

Toast your sourdough and spread with butter. Spoon the eggs on top, then flake the kipper on top (discarding the skin). Scatter with a little parsley and serve with lemon wedges.

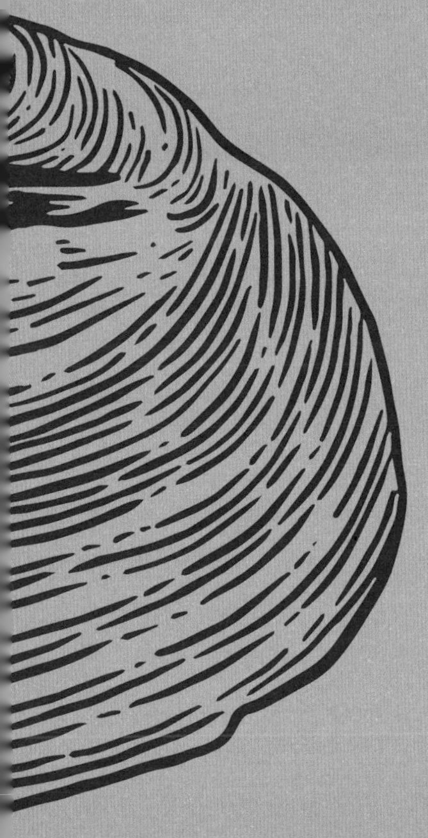

Cheesy Toasts

Tuna melt

SERVES **2**

PREPARATION TIME **5 MINUTES**

COOKING TIME **12 MINUTES**

This is (literally) melt-in-your-mouth delicious. Using mayo on the outside of the bread gives a perfect crispy finish, and the cheese becomes completely molten. If you're a fan of a little heat, I'd really recommend the jalapeño addition.

200g (7oz) tin of tuna in brine, drained
1 spring onion, finely chopped
1 tsp Dijon mustard
4 tbsp mayonnaise
1 tbsp capers, drained roughly chopped
½ tsp chopped dill fronds
100g (3½oz) Cheddar
4 slices of granary bread
jalapeño relish (optional), to serve

Combine the tuna, spring onion, Dijon mustard, 2 tablespoons of mayonnaise, the capers and chopped dill in a bowl.

Use the remaining 2 tablespoons of mayonnaise to spread over one side of each piece of bread. Spoon the tuna mayo onto two of the pieces of bread (the un-mayoed side) and then top with the cheese, followed by the other piece of bread (mayo-side out).

Heat a non-stick wide-based frying pan over a medium-high heat. Add the sandwiches, with the cheese side facing down so it can start to melt and meld together. Cook for about 6 minutes, pushing down slightly with the back of a fish slice. Carefully flip and cook for another 5–6 minutes. Serve!

Tip For an added kick, add some jalapeño relish to the middle of the sandwich. Perfect.

Baked feta with honey and thyme

SERVES **4**

PREPARATION TIME **5 MINUTES**

COOKING TIME **20 MINUTES**

I think I could eat a whole block of this myself! The outside is crunchy and caramelized and the inside molten and creamy, swimming in a pool of sweetened oil. Heaven. The chilli is subtle, just adding a little warm kick to this salty cheese, and it's the perfect little sharing plate to start a meal!

200g (7oz) block of feta
1 tbsp extra virgin olive oil
1½ tbsp honey
3 sprigs of thyme, leaves picked
¼ tsp chilli flakes
toasted pitta, flatbread or sourdough, to serve

Preheat the oven to 200°C fan (450°F/gas 8).

Put the block of feta into a shallow heatproof dish. Drizzle the olive oil over the feta, followed by the honey, thyme leaves and chilli flakes. Bake for 15–18 minutes until golden and bubbling. Place in the middle of the table and serve with toasted breads to pile the golden feta onto.

Welsh rarebit

SERVES **2**

PREPARATION TIME **10 MINUTES**

COOKING TIME **15 MINUTES**

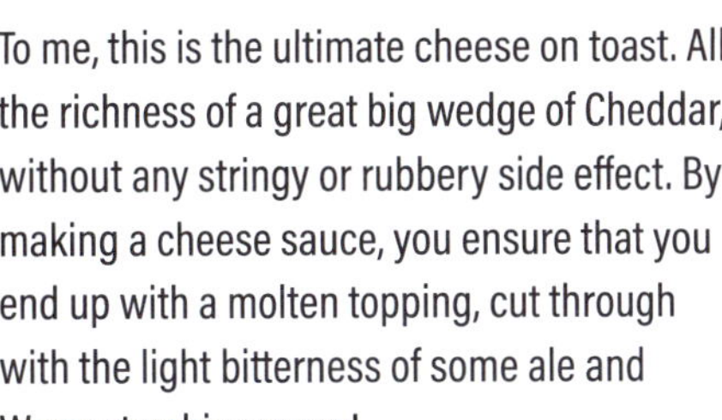

To me, this is the ultimate cheese on toast. All the richness of a great big wedge of Cheddar, without any stringy or rubbery side effect. By making a cheese sauce, you ensure that you end up with a molten topping, cut through with the light bitterness of some ale and Worcestershire sauce!

25g (¾oz) salted butter
25g (¾oz) plain flour
100ml (3½fl oz) brown ale
160g Cheddar, grated
1 tsp mustard powder
1 tsp Worcestershire sauce
2 large slices of white or wholemeal sourdough

Put a medium saucepan over a medium heat. Add the butter and melt, then add the flour and mix to combine to a paste. Gradually add the ale, mixing to make a smooth sauce. Add the cheese and mustard powder, and stir gently over a low heat until melted. Add the Worcestershire sauce and remove from the heat.

Heat a grill to medium-high. Toast the bread on one side until golden. Put toasted-side down onto a baking tray and spoon the cheese mixture on top. Return to the grill until bubbling and golden.

Roasted grape and brie

SERVES **2**

PREPARATION TIME **10 MINUTES**

COOKING TIME **10 MINUTES**

Fruit and brie are an undisputable combo, and the sweetness of the roasted grapes and shallot here make the most delectable accompaniment to the creamy French cheese.

200g (7oz) red grapes on their vine
2 banana shallots, thinly sliced
1 tbsp olive oil
1 sprig of rosemary, leaves picked
2 slices of seeded sourdough, or bread of your choice
120g (4oz) brie, thickly sliced
20g (¾oz) walnuts
flaky sea salt and freshly ground black pepper

Preheat the oven to 180°C fan (375°F/gas 5) and line a baking sheet with baking parchment.

Put the grapes onto the prepared sheet with the sliced shallot. Drizzle with the oil and scatter with the rosemary. Season with salt and pepper. Put in the oven and cook for 8 minutes.

While it is cooking, lightly toast your bread in a toaster, then top with the brie. When the grapes have cooked for 8 minutes, put the brie on toast on another baking sheet and cook both for another 8 minutes, adding the walnuts to the tray with the brie for the final 3 minutes. Allow the walnuts to cool slightly before roughly chopping. Use a fork to pull the grapes away from their vine. Top the brie on toast with the grapes and shallot, then scatter with the chopped walnuts and a good grind of black pepper.

French onion toast

SERVES **2**

PREPARATION TIME **5 MINUTES**

COOKING TIME **30 MINUTES**

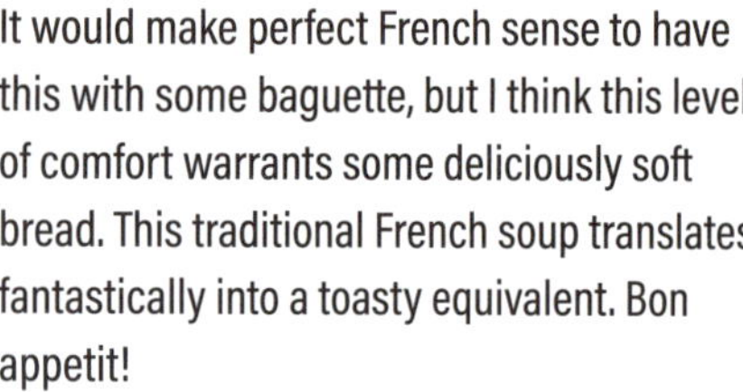

It would make perfect French sense to have this with some baguette, but I think this level of comfort warrants some deliciously soft bread. This traditional French soup translates fantastically into a toasty equivalent. Bon appetit!

1 tbsp butter
1 tbsp olive oil
2 onions, thinly sliced
1 tsp caster sugar
2 garlic cloves, crushed
4 sprigs of thyme, leaves picked, plus extra to serve
1 tbsp brandy (optional)
2 tsp plain flour
250ml (9fl oz) beef stock
½ tbsp Worcestershire sauce
50g (2oz) Gruyère, grated
2 large slices of fresh white bread
freshly ground black pepper

Heat the butter and olive oil in a large, wide-based frying pan. Add the onions and cook over a medium-high heat for 20 minutes until super-softened, sticky and starting to colour. Sprinkle in the sugar with the garlic and cook for another minute, before adding the thyme. Add the brandy, if using, and allow to cook off, before adding the flour and stirring through the onions. Gradually add the stock and Worcestershire sauce and cook for 4–5 minutes until thickened but still saucy. Toast the bread and preheat the grill. Put the toasted bread onto a baking tray and top with the juicy onions and then scatter with the Gruyère. Pop under the grill and cook for 4–5 minutes until melted and golden . Serve scattered with a little extra thyme and grind of black pepper.

Blue cheese and mushrooms

SERVES **2**

PREPARATION TIME **10 MINUTES**

COOKING TIME **15 MINUTES**

Blue cheese and mushrooms are a perfect pairing – the saltiness of the cheese really heightens the flavour of the mushrooms. By chucking it all under the grill, you end up with an amazing ooziness.

1 tbsp olive oil
300g (10½oz) chestnut mushrooms, sliced
2 sprigs of thyme, leaves picked
2 garlic cloves crushed
60g (2¼oz) cream cheese
100g (3½oz) blue cheese, crumbled
2 slices of granary bread, toasted
extra thyme leaves, to serve

Put a wide-based non-stick frying pan over a medium-high heat. Add the olive oil and heat. Add the mushrooms and cook for 8–10 minutes, increasing the heat towards the end to evaporate any moisture, if necessary. Add the thyme and garlic and fry for another 30 seconds, then remove from the heat and stir through the cream cheese and half the blue cheese.

Preheat the grill. Place the toast onto a baking tray. Top with the mushrooms, then crumble the remaining blue cheese on top. Pop under the grill for 4–5 minutes until golden and bubbling. Finish with a scattering of thyme.

Feta with tomatoes and pepper

SERVES **4**

PREPARATION TIME **5 MINUTES**

COOKING TIME **25 MINUTES**

This is based on a classic dish from northern Greece. The tomatoes and peppers roast and sweeten, starting to break down, while the feta gets creamier and caramelized. It's a deliciously easy and cozy meal.

200g (7oz) cherry tomatoes, halved
1 pointed sweet pepper, deseeded and chopped
2 garlic cloves, crushed
½ tbsp white wine vinegar
1 red chilli, deseeded and chopped
200g (7oz) feta, broken into chunks
1 tsp dried oregano
1 tbsp extra virgin olive oil, plus extra to serve
2 Greek flatbreads, cut in half
flaky sea salt and freshly ground black pepper

Preheat the oven to 200°C fan (450°F/gas 8).

Put the tomatoes, pepper and crushed garlic onto the base of a baking dish. Toss together with the vinegar and some seasoning. Scatter with the chilli and then the feta, topping with the dried oregano and then drizzling with the olive oil. Cover with aluminium foil and bake for 15 minutes. Remove the foil and cook for another 10 minutes.

Toast the flatbreads. Serve the feta piled onto the flatbreads, finished with a final drizzle of oil.

Leek and tallegio

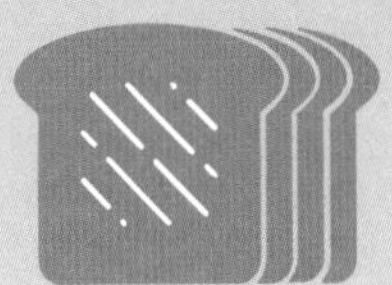

SERVES **4**

PREPARATION TIME **5 MINUTES**

COOKING TIME **30 MINUTES**

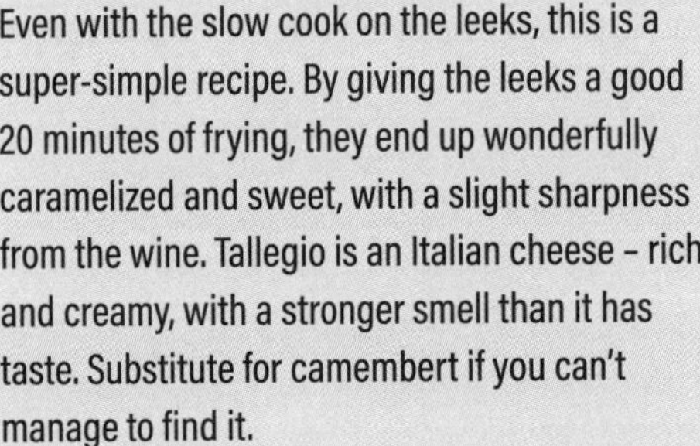

Even with the slow cook on the leeks, this is a super-simple recipe. By giving the leeks a good 20 minutes of frying, they end up wonderfully caramelized and sweet, with a slight sharpness from the wine. Tallegio is an Italian cheese – rich and creamy, with a stronger smell than it has taste. Substitute for camembert if you can't manage to find it.

2 tbsp olive oil
2 tbsp butter
2 leeks, cleaned and thinly sliced
6 sprigs of thyme, leaves picked
125ml white wine
4 slices of sourdough, lightly toasted
200g (7oz) tallegio or camembert, cut into thick slices
1 lemon, cut into wedges

Put the oil and butter in a heavy-based non-stick frying pan over a medium heat and add the leeks. Cook for 20–25 minutes until sticky and browned. Add the thyme and wine and cook for another couple of minutes until the liquid has evaporated. Load onto the toast, then top with the tallegio slices. Place under a preheated grill until part-melted. Squeeze over the lemon wedges to serve.

Goats cheese with fig relish

SERVES **2**

PREPARATION TIME **5 MINUTES**

COOKING TIME **30 MINUTES**

Fig and goats' cheese are a classic pairing, but by simmering the fruit down into a relish with some brown sugar and vinegar, you get an amazing acidity to cut through the rich and creamy cheese. The chilli level is subtle, so you can always add extra if you want more kick.

1 tbsp olive oil
1 small red onion, finely chopped
1 red chilli, deseeded and finely diced
2 garlic cloves, crushed
280g fresh figs (8 medium), roughly chopped
70ml white wine vinegar
50g soft brown sugar
6 sprigs thyme, leaves picked
4 small pieces of wholemeal sourdough
150g (5oz) goats' cheese (skin-on), cut into 8 pieces
flaky sea salt and freshly ground black pepper
handful of dressed rocket, to serve

Put the olive oil in a medium saucepan over a medium heat and add the onion. Fry for 8–10 minutes until softened. Add the chilli and garlic and fry for another 30 seconds, then add the figs, white wine vinegar and brown sugar. Simmer for 4–5 minutes until the sugar has dissolved and the figs have started to break down. Increase the heat slightly and bring to a rapid simmer for 3–5 minutes until thickened. Remove from the heat. Stir through half the thyme leaves.

Preheat the grill to high. Put the bread on a baking tray and put under the grill until golden. Remove from the oven and turn, toasted side down. Spoon the fig relish on top, followed by the goats' cheese. Put under the grill until the goats' cheese is golden and bubbling. Give a good grind of black pepper, scatter with the remaining thyme and serve with dressed rocket leaves on the side.

Aubergine parmigiana

SERVES **2**

PREPARATION TIME **10 MINUTES**

COOKING TIME **20 MINUTES**

This Italian staple is rich and substantial, without any need for meat. With the layer of molten cheese, it's definitely a comfort food. It's a popular Italian sandwich filling, so topping toast with it isn't too much of a stretch of the imagination.

5 tbsp olive oil
1 aubergine, cut into 1cm (½in) discs
400g (14oz) chopped tomatoes
2 tbsp tomato purée
3 garlic cloves, crushed
1 tsp caster sugar
1 tbsp white wine vinegar
2 large pieces of focaccia or white bread
125g (4oz) mozzarella (drained weight), drained on kitchen paper
20g (¾oz) parmesan, finely grated (vegetarian, if liked)

Set a large, heavy-based frying pan over a medium-high heat. Add 4 tablespoons of the olive oil and, once hot, add the aubergine and cook for 3–4 minutes on each side until golden. You may need to do this in batches. Transfer the aubergine to a chopping board.

Lower the temperature under the pan and add the final tablespoon of olive oil, followed by the chopped tomatoes, tomato purée, garlic, sugar and vinegar. Bring to a simmer, then return the aubergine to the pan and gently coat in the tomato sauce. Cook for 5–6 minutes until the sauce has thickened, stirring occasionally.

Preheat the grill and lightly toast the bread. Load the aubergines onto the toast and shred the mozzarella on top, followed by a scattering of parmesan. Put under the grill until the cheese is bubbling and golden.

Braised leeks, gribiche and wensleydale

SERVES **2**

PREPARATION TIME **10 MINUTES**

COOKING TIME **30 MINUTES**

Gribiche is a cold egg sauce (tastier than it sounds) – somewhere between egg mayonnaise and a homemade mayonnaise! It's a perfect base here for the caramelized leeks and delicious shavings of Wensleydale. If you can't find Wensleydale, feta would be a saltier substitute, or you could go for a mild Cheddar.

2 eggs
1 tbsp olive oil
2 medium leeks, trimmed and halved lengthways and any tough outer leaves removed
100ml (3½fl oz) white wine
300ml (10fl oz) chicken or vegetable stock
1 tbsp Dijon mustard
1 tbsp white wine vinegar
1 tbsp grapeseed oil
2 tbsp extra virgin olive oil
1 tbsp capers, drained and roughly chopped
about 6 mini cornichons, roughly chopped
4 sprigs of tarragon, leaves stripped and roughly chopped
1½ tbsp roughly chopped parsley leaves
40g (1½oz) Wensleydale, shaved
2 pieces of wholemeal bread
flaky sea salt and freshly ground black pepper

Put the eggs in a pan of boiling water and cook for 9 minutes. Remove to a bowl of cold water and leave to cool completely.

Meanwhile, put a wide-based, non-stick frying pan over a medium-high heat. Add the olive oil, then the leeks, cut side-down, and cook for about 3 minutes until dark golden. Flip and do the same on the other side. Return to the cut side, add the wine and cook to reduce to a thick sauce before adding the stock. Bring to the boil, then reduce to a gently simmer and cook for 10–15 minutes until the leeks are tender.

Meanwhile, make the gribiche. Halve the cooled eggs and put the yolks in a bowl. Mash the yolks, then add the Dijon mustard and mix until smooth. Whisk in the vinegar, grapeseed oil and extra virgin olive oil. Finely chop the egg whites and fold into the mixture with the capers, cornichons and herbs. Season with salt and pepper to taste.

Toast the bread, then top with the gribiche. Remove the leeks to a chopping board and cut in half. Pile onto the toasts and top with the Wensleydale.

Reuben sandwich

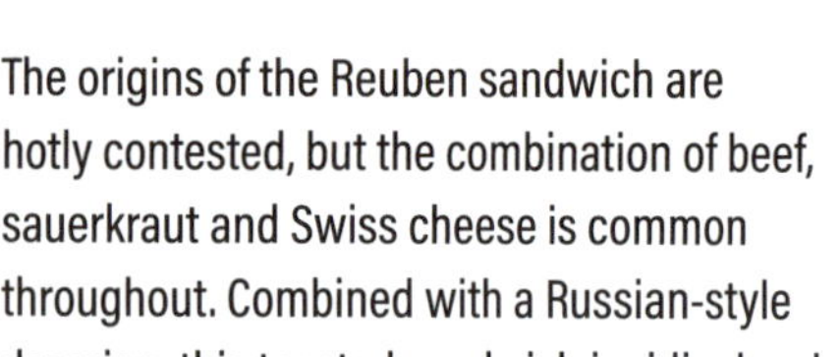

SERVES **2**

PREPARATION TIME **5 MINUTES**

COOKING TIME **10-12 MINUTES**

The origins of the Reuben sandwich are hotly contested, but the combination of beef, sauerkraut and Swiss cheese is common throughout. Combined with a Russian-style dressing, this toasted sandwich is ridiculously mouthwatering.

FOR THE DRESSING

2 tbsp mayonnaise
1 tbsp tomato ketchup
1 tsp horseradish
1 tsp Dijon mustard
1 small shallot, finely chopped
20g (¾oz) mini gherkins, finely chopped, plus extra gherkins, to serve
2 tsp gherkin brine

FOR THE SANDWICH

4 slices of rye sourdough
butter, for spreading
10 slices of pastrami (or 100g/3½oz, depending on size of pastrami)
80g (3oz) sauerkraut
75g (2½oz) Gruyère, grated

Start by making the dressing. Combine all the ingredients in a bowl.

Butter both sides of each piece of bread. Spread most of the dressing on one side of two pieces (save any leftover to serve with the sandwich). Lay the pastrami on the dressing, followed by the sauerkraut, then the Gruyère. Top with the other slices of bread.

Heat a wide-based, non-stick frying pan over a medium-high heat. Pan-fry for 5-6 minutes, then turn and fry for another 5–6 minutes. Slice to serve, with extra pickles on the side, and the leftover dressing to dip crusts.

Croque monsieur

SERVES **4**

PREPARATION TIME **10 MINUTES**

COOKING TIME **20 MINUTES**

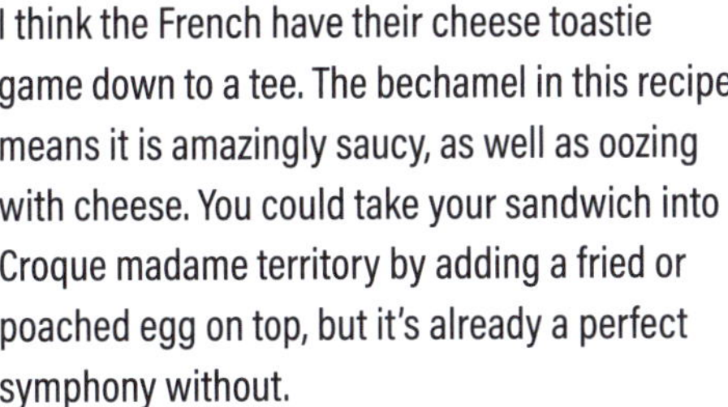

I think the French have their cheese toastie game down to a tee. The bechamel in this recipe means it is amazingly saucy, as well as oozing with cheese. You could take your sandwich into Croque madame territory by adding a fried or poached egg on top, but it's already a perfect symphony without.

30g (1oz) unsalted butter
30g (1oz) plain flour
280ml (9fl oz) whole milk
170g (6oz) mature Cheddar, grated
170g (6oz) Comte cheese, grated
8 medium-thin slices of sourdough
2 tbsp Dijon mustard
8 slices of ham (French, if possible)

Preheat the oven to 175°C fan (350°F/gas 4).

Set a saucepan over a medium heat and add the butter and flour. Whisk with a balloon whisk until it comes together to form a paste, then slowly add the milk, whisking to combine and thicken. Remove from the heat.

Combine the Comte cheese and Cheddar in a large bowl, then add 75g (½oz) to the white sauce and stir to combine. Lightly toast the bread. Lay 4 pieces of toast on a lined baking tray. Spread the mustard onto them, then spread with 2 tablespoons of bechamel sauce per slice. Divide the ham between the slices, folding the ham to fit your bread, then top with half the cheese. Top with the other halves of the toast, then spread with the remaining bechamel, finishing with the remaining cheese. Put in the oven and bake for 15 minutes until the cheese is bubbling and golden.

Burrata and Parma ham with griddled peach

SERVES **2**

PREPARATION TIME **5 MINUTES**

COOKING TIME **10 MINUTES**

This Italian-inspired recipe is the absolute epitome of summer dining. It makes plenty of dressing, so other ingredients could easily be doubled to serve as part of an al fresco build-your-own meal.

½ red chilli, deseeded and finely chopped
1 garlic clove, crushed
3 tbsp extra virgin olive oil
1 tbsp honey
1 tsp Dijon mustard
1 tbsp white wine vinegar
flaky sea salt and freshly ground black pepper
1 flat or round peach, sliced
12cm (4½in) piece of ciabatta, cut in half
a handful of rocket
4 slices of Parma ham
1 ball of burrata, 150g (5oz) drained weight

Put the chilli and garlic in a heatproof bowl. Heat 2 tablespoons of the olive oil in a frying pan. When hot, pour over the chilli and garlic in the bowl, before stirring in the honey, mustard and vinegar. Season with salt and pepper, then mix to combine.

Place a griddle over a high heat. Add the peach slices and cook for about 2½ minutes on each side until charred. Set aside.

Add the remaining 1 tablespoon of olive oil to the frying pan and set over a medium-high heat . Add the ciabatta, cut-side down, and fry for 3–4 minutes until golden. Top the golden ciabatta with some rocket and 2 pieces of Parma ham per slice. Divide the burrata between the plates and top with the peach slices, then the dressing!

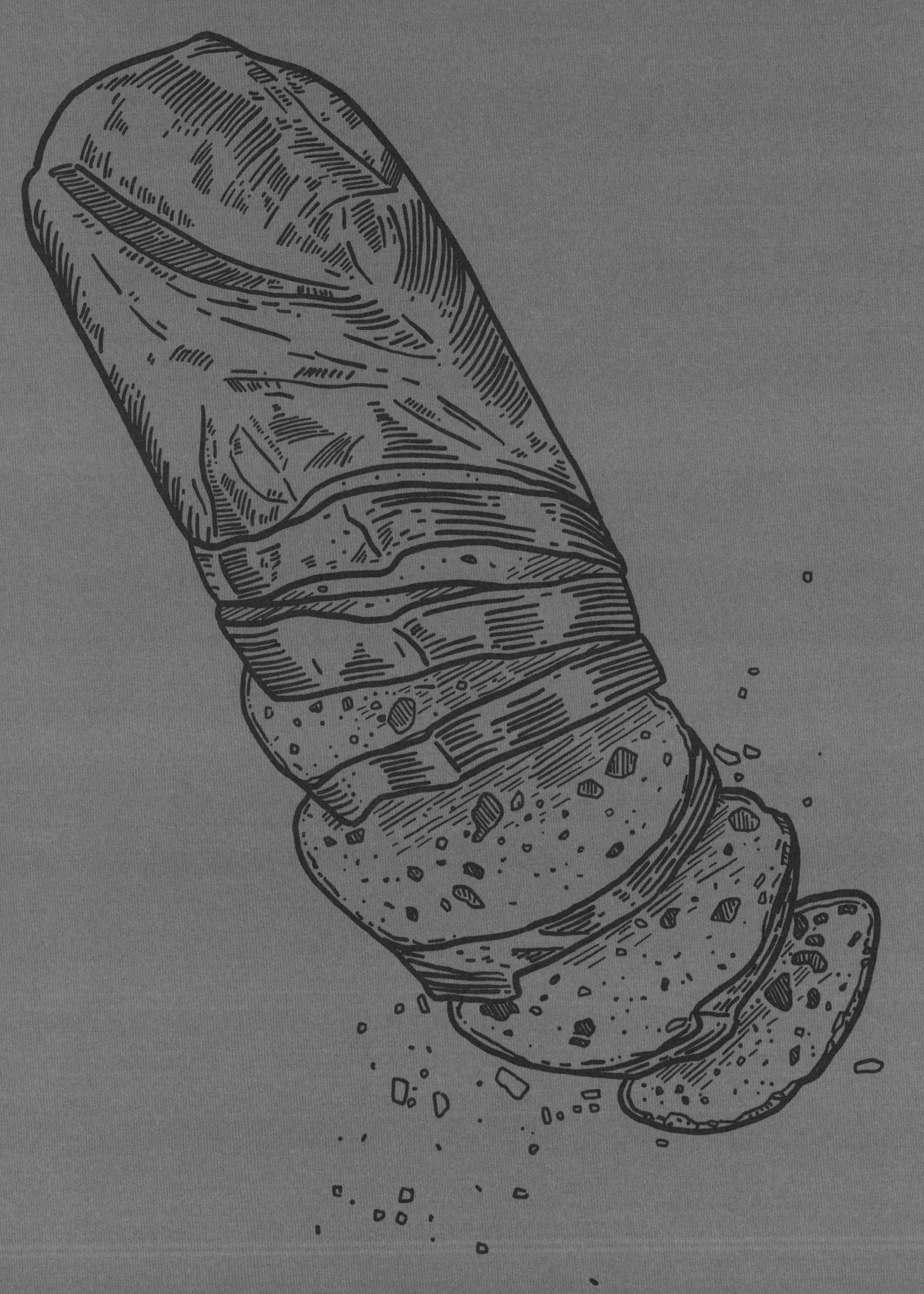

Meals on Toast

Steak with sticky horseradish onions

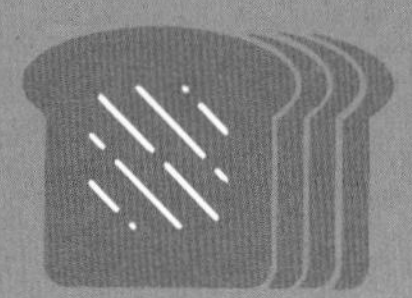

SERVES **2**

PREPARATION TIME **10 MINUTES**

COOKING TIME **20 MINUTES**

Adding horseradish and mustard to these caramelized onions makes them the perfect partner to the succulent steak. It's an indulgent open sandwich dinner, that would be great with some shoestring fries, or crisps, on the side. You can buy crispy onions in tubs if time is short, or simply fry your own.

2 tbsp olive oil
1 onion, thinly sliced
1 tsp caster sugar
1 tbsp white wine vinegar
1 tbsp wholegrain mustard
2 tbsp horseradish sauce
2 x 225g (8oz) sirloin steaks (at room temperature for at least an hour before cooking)
1 white demi-baguette, cut in half horizontally
2 tbsp mayonnaise
30g (1oz) rocket
1 tbsp crispy onions
flaky sea salt and freshly ground black pepper

Heat 1 tablespoon of olive oil in a frying pan and cook the onions over a medium heat for 10–12 minutes until softened and sticky. Then add the sugar and vinegar and cook for another 2 minutes before turning off the heat and stirring through the mustard and horseradish.

Meanwhile, heat a large, non-stick frying pan over a high heat. Add the remaining tablespoon of olive oil. When hot, season the steaks with salt and pepper, then add to the pan. Cook for 2–2½ minutes on each side (for medium rare), and an extra 2 minutes rendering the fat on the side, if you want to eat it. Set aside on a chopping board to rest for 10 minutes, then slice.

Return the steak pan to a medium heat. Add the baguette, cut-side down, and cook for a couple of minutes until lightly golden. Spread the toasted baguette with mayonnaise. Spoon the horseradish onions on top, followed by a scattering of rocket, then the steak. Top with a sprinkle of crispy onions.

Fish fingers with tartare

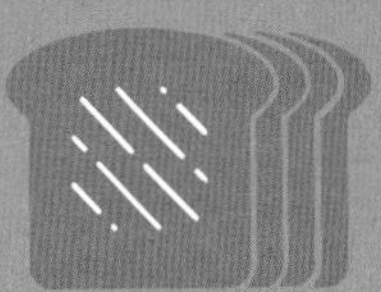

SERVES **2**

PREPARATION TIME **15 MINUTES**

COOKING TIME **10 MINUTES**

I love fish with vinegary, salty tartare sauce. I also love fish with lemon and ketchup (or most things with ketchup!). I was aiming for a fancy fish finger open-sandwich situation here, but ketchup came knocking and I wasn't sad when it joined the party. You could even take it up a notch by melting burger cheese onto your bread when it's hot straight out of the toaster.

75g (2½oz) mayonnaise
2 tbsp capers, drained and roughly chopped
30g (1oz) cornichons, roughly chopped
1 tbsp finely chopped parsley
1 lemon, one half juiced and zested
30g (1oz) plain flour
1 egg
40g (1½oz) panko breadcrumbs
15g (½oz) parmesan, finely grated
225g (8oz) cod loin
1 tbsp sunflower oil
2 slices of multiseed bread
flaky sea salt and freshly ground black pepper
tomato ketchup, to serve (optional)

Make the tartare sauce by combining the mayonnaise, capers, cornichons, parsley and the juice of ½ lemon in a bowl. Season with salt and pepper and mix to combine.

Put the plain flour into a shallow bowl. Season with salt and pepper.

Crack the egg into another bowl, and lightly whisk with some seasoning.

Put the panko breadcrumbs into a shallow bowl along with the parmesan and lemon zest. Season with salt and pepper.

Pat dry the cod fillets then cut each into four strips. Dip in the flour mixture, then into the egg, before finishing in the panko mixture.

Put a heavy-based non-stick frying pan over a medium-high heat. Add the oil and, once hot, add the fish fingers. Pan-fry for about 1½ minutes on each of the four sides, until they're golden and the fish inside is opaque and cooked through.

Toast the bread and spread half the tartare on each piece, then pop four fish fingers on each slice. Drizzle with the remaining sauce (and ketchup, if using) and the lemon half, cut into wedges, on the side.

Seven-spiced lamb with tahini and pomegranate

SERVES **4**

PREPARATION TIME **10 MINUTES**

COOKING TIME **15 MINUTES**

This Lebanese spice mix is a quick and tasty way to add some delicious flavours to your fried lamb. It's an easy and impressive 15-minute meal.

1 tbsp olive oil
1 onion, chopped
3 garlic cloves, crushed
500g (1lb 2oz) minced lamb
2 tsp Lebanese seven spice
2 tbsp tomato purée
1 tbsp honey
2 tbsp roughly chopped mint leaves
a handful of coriander, leaves picked and chopped, stalks finely chopped
a handful of parsley, leaves picked and roughly chopped, stalks finely chopped
2 tbsp tahini
juice of 1 lemon
Lebanese flatbreads
80g (3oz) pomegranate seeds
flaky sea salt and freshly ground black pepper

Heat the olive oil in a wide-based frying pan over a medium-high heat. Add the onion and cook for 8 minutes. Add 2 cloves of crushed garlic and cook for another minute until fragrant. Add the minced lamb and seven spice, increase the heat and cook for 5–6 minutes. Add the tomato purée and honey with 50ml (2fl oz) of water. Cook through for another minute, then remove from the heat. Stir through half the herb leaves and all the stalks.

Mix the remaining garlic clove with the tahini and lemon juice in a small bowl. Slowly whisk in 2 tablespoons of water. Season with salt and pepper.

Toast the flatbreads and top with the lamb. Drizzle with the tahini dressing, then scatter with the herbs and pomegranate seeds.

Miso salmon with Asian-style slaw

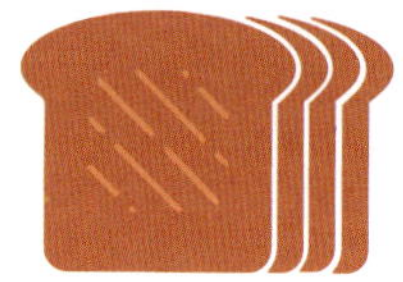

SERVES **2**

PREPARATION TIME **10 MINUTES, PLUS OPTIONAL MARINATING**

COOKING TIME **10 MINUTES**

Zingy slaw and slightly blackened tender miso salmon – this meal on toast is simultaneously light and also comforting.

2½ tbsp white miso
1 tbsp honey
1 tbsp light soy sauce
1½ tbsp rice vinegar
2 x 125g (4oz) salmon fillets
zest and juice of 1 lime
1 tbsp ginger and garlic paste
1 tbsp toasted sesame oil
1 tbsp kewpie or regular mayonnaise
1 large carrot, grated or julienned
¼ small red cabbage, shredded or mandolined
1 tbsp sunflower oil
2 slices of bread (wholegrain works nicely)
coriander leaves, to serve

Combine the miso, honey, soy sauce and ½ tablespoon of rice vinegar in a small bowl. Put the salmon fillets onto a plate and spread the flesh side with 2 tablespoons of the miso mixture, reserving the rest. Set the salmon aside while you prepare the slaw (or marinate for a couple of hours, if you have time).

Combine the lime zest and juice, ginger and garlic paste, sesame oil, mayonnaise and remaining rice vinegar in a bowl. Add the carrot and cabbage and mix to thoroughly combine.

Heat the sunflower oil in a medium non-stick frying pan over a medium-high heat. Add the salmon, skin-side down, and cook for 3 minutes. Turn and cook on one of the edges for 1 minute, before turning onto its full flesh side to cook for 3 more minutes. Then finish with 1 minute on the final face. The salmon will be a little pink when finished, so cook a bit longer if you prefer it well cooked. Add 1 tablespoon of boiling water to the remaining miso marinade, if needed, to loosen it.

Toast your bread. Pile the slaw on top. Flake the salmon, cutting through the skin, and load on top of the slaw. Drizzle with the remaining sauce and finish with some coriander leaves.

Masala chickpeas

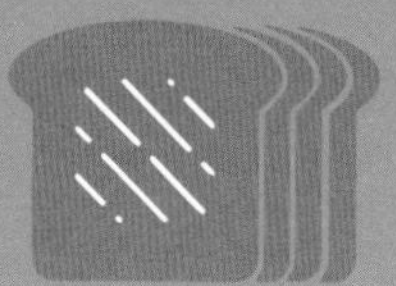

SERVES 4

PREPARATION TIME 10 MINUTES, PLUS SOAKING

COOKING TIME 25 MINUTES

This recipe pays homage to a comforting and lightly spiced Indian chickpea curry – chana masala. Paratha is a wonderfully buttery, flaky bread, which you can buy frozen to pan-fry at home. The luscious layers are an amazing base for the balanced vegetarian curry and the sweet and sour date and tamarind sauce.

4 pitted medjool dates, roughly chopped
75ml (2½fl oz) tamarind sauce (if using tamarind paste, add ½ tsp each of ground ginger and chilli powder)
2 tbsp sunflower oil
1 onion, chopped
1 tbsp ground cumin
1 tbsp ground coriander
1 tsp turmeric
5 garlic cloves, crushed
15g (½oz) piece of ginger root, peeled and grated
1 green chilli, finely chopped
400g (14oz) chopped tomatoes
570g (1lb 4½oz) jar of chickpeas, drained (400g/14oz drained weight)
2 tbsp roughly chopped coriander leaves
1 tsp garam masala
4 paratha, or mini naan
salted butter, for spreading, at room temperature

To start, soak the dates in 75ml (2½fl oz) of boiling water for 10 minutes. Add the tamarind sauce and blitz until smooth.

Set a medium non-stick frying pan over a medium-high heat. Add the oil, followed by the onion, and cook for 8 minutes. Add the ground cumin, ground coriander and turmeric, followed by the garlic, ginger and chilli. Fry for couple of minutes until fragrant. Add the tomatoes and chickpeas, with 200ml (7fl oz) of water. Simmer for 15 minutes until thickened. Stir through half the coriander leaves and the garam masala, loosening with a little extra water, if needed.

Pan-fry the paratha (or toast the naan) and then spread with a little butter. Top with the chana masala and drizzle with the chutney and a final scatter of coriander.

Celeriac remoulade and ham hock

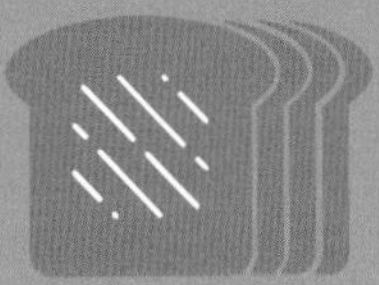

SERVES **4**

PREPARATION TIME **15 MINUTES**

Celeriac is a great alternative to a traditional slaw, with more complex nutty and fennely undertones. Topped with ham hock, it is a simple and delicious toast-topper.

1 lemon
2 tbsp Dijon mustard
150g (5oz) mayonnaise
½ celeriac (about 400g/14oz)
4 slices of wholemeal sourdough
salted butter, for spreading
150g (5oz) good-quality shredded ham hock
1 tbsp chopped parsley

Juice the lemon into a small bowl, reserving the lemon 'shell'. Add the mustard and mayonnaise to the lemon juice, and mix to combine. Add the lemon shells to a large bowl and top up with cold water. Peel the celeriac and then very thinly slice (on a mandolin if you have one) and then cut into very thin matchsticks, adding them to the bowl of water as you go so that the celeriac doesn't discolour. When it's all prepped, drain thoroughly and discard the lemon halves. Pat the celeriac dry on kitchen paper or a clean tea towel, then return to the dry bowl and stir in the dressing. Leave to sit for an hour.

Toast the bread then spread with butter. Load up with the celeriac, spooning over the resting juices. Top with the ham hock and scatter with parsley to serve.

Chicory and samphire with rollmop herring

SERVES **4**

PREPARATION TIME **10 MINUTES**

COOKING TIME **2 MINUTES**

Salty pops of samphire and the bitter chicory leaves in a punchy mustard dressing go excellently with rollmop. This iconic pickled herring makes a great fridge staple for some mouth-smacking acidity (countered with some delicious crème fraîche!).

2½ tbsp extra virgin olive oil
90g (3¼oz) samphire
2 tsp Dijon mustard
1 tbsp white wine vinegar
2 small red chicory, roughly sliced
4 slices of rye, or wheat and rye, bread
4 tbsp crème fraîche
4 ready-to-eat rollmop herrings, each sliced into 4
1 tbsp chopped parsley

Set a frying pan over a medium-high heat. Add ½ tablespoon of olive oil, then the samphire. Cook for 2 minutes, then remove to a plate. Mix the remaining olive oil with the mustard and vinegar in a large bowl, then toss through the chicory leaves. Toast the rye bread, then spread with the crème fraîche. Divide the samphire and chicory salad between the toasts, before topping with a rollmop and a scattering of parsley.

Mussels with chorizo and broad beans

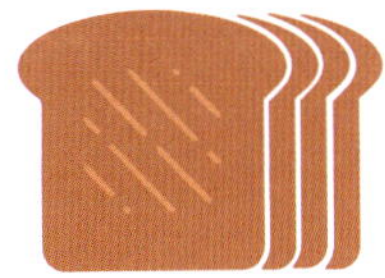

SERVES **2**

PREPARATION TIME **5 MINUTES**

COOKING TIME **15 MINUTES**

Mussels are the kind of food that rely heavily on the strength of their surroundings – and the chorizo and cream here are doing some pretty decent legwork. Using de-shelled mussels means there's minimal fuss, and all the cooking juices are able to soak into the lightly garlicky toast.

100g (3½oz) chorizo, diced into rough 1cm (½in) chunks
3 garlic cloves, 2 sliced and 1 halved
100ml (3½fl oz) white wine
(3½oz) frozen broad beans
200g (7oz) mussels out of their shells (fresh or defrosted, as per pack instructions)
75ml (2½fl oz) double cream
1½ tbsp roughly chopped parsley
2 slices of sourdough

Set a medium non-stick pan over a medium-high heat. Add the chorizo and fry for 5–6 minutes until crisped and releasing its oils. Reduce the heat and add the garlic, continuing to fry for another 1½–2 minutes until fragrant. Add the wine and bubble for 2 minutes until reduced slightly, then stir through the broad beans and cook for another 1½ minutes. Stir through the mussels with the double cream and bubble briefly to heat through. Remove from the heat and stir through the parsley. Toast the sourdough and rub with the cut garlic clove. Pile the mussels and chorizo on top of the toast, with all the pan juices.

Satay-style chicken with coriander relish

SERVES **4**

PREPARATION TIME **10 MINUTES, PLUS MARINADING**

COOKING TIME **20 MINUTES**

This south-east Asian-inspired chicken dish is a wonderful balance of sweetness, saltiness, acidity and creaminess. It's pretty easy prep for a lot of flavour. Charring the chicken on the griddle really adds to the dish – so it's worth a little extra effort with the cooking process.

FOR THE SAUCE

50g (2oz) piece of ginger root, peeled and grated
zest and juices of 2 limes
4 garlic cloves, crushed
2 tbsp soy sauce
3 tbsp runny peanut butter
2 tbsp honey
2 tsp ground coriander
2 tsp ground cumin
1 tsp turmeric
160ml (5½fl oz) coconut cream
flaky sea salt and freshly ground black pepper

FOR THE CHICKEN

6 chicken thighs, boned but with skin-on
2 tsp caster sugar
3 tbsp white wine vinegar
2 tbsp finely chopped coriander leaves
4 wholemeal chapati or slices of wholemeal bread

Mix all the sauce ingredients in a large bowl, then season with salt and pepper. Spoon half into a small saucepan and add the chicken to the bowl, turning to fully coat it. Marinate the chicken for 20 minutes.

Put 50ml (2fl oz) of water in the saucepan with the sauce and simmer for 5 minutes over a medium heat while you prepare the chicken.

Preheat the griddle to medium-high and cook the chicken for about 7 minutes on each side until the meat is cooked through and the skin is dark golden. Meanwhile, combine the caster sugar and vinegar in a small bowl and mix to dissolve the sugar. Stir in the coriander.

When cooked, transfer the chicken to a chopping board and slice. Fry the chapati or toast the bread. Drizzle with the peanut sauce then pile on the chicken, followed by more sauce. Finally, spoon some coriander relish over the top.

Roasted squash with labneh and tarragon agrodolce

SERVES **2**

PREPARATION TIME **10 MINUTES, PLUS OVERNIGHT LABNEH STRAINING**

COOKING TIME **25 MINUTES**

Golden brown and caramelized, the smell of the roasted butternut squash with cinnamon really makes this dish mouthwatering. Sandwiched between some rich labneh and a sharp but sweet agrodolce, it's the kind of recipe you'll happily want to add to your entertaining repertoire.

400g (14oz) Greek yogurt
½ tsp salt
½ butternut squash, deseeded and cut into rough 5mm (¼in) thick slices
1 tbsp olive oil
½ tsp ground cinnamon
40g (1½oz) honey
50ml (2fl oz) sherry vinegar
1 tsp chilli flakes (Aleppo, if possible)
1 garlic clove, crushed
1 tbsp chopped tarragon leaves
1 tbsp extra virgin olive oil
20g (¾oz) mixed seeds
flaky sea salt and freshly ground black pepper
4 slices of whichever bread you fancy

To make the labneh, line a bowl with muslin, then pour in the yogurt and salt and tie up the muslin. Suspend it over a bowl and refrigerate overnight to drain off any excess moisture.

Preheat the oven to 200°C fan (450°F/gas 8).

Put the squash on a baking tray, drizzle with the olive oil and scatter with the cinnamon. Season with salt and pepper, then roast for 25 minutes.

Meanwhile, combine the honey, vinegar and chilli flakes in a small saucepan and set over a simmering heat for 5–6 minutes until syrupy. Stir in the garlic and tarragon and leave to infuse.

Heat the extra virgin olive oil in a small frying pan over a medium-high heat. Add the seeds and toast for around 5 minutes until golden and popping. Season with flaky salt.

Toast the bread. Loosen the dressing with a little water if needed. Spread the bread with the labneh and top with the squash. Scatter with the seeds and then drizzle with the dressing.

Steak and garlic and tomato confit with a chimichurri sauce

SERVES **2**

PREPARATION TIME **20 MINUTES**

COOKING TIME **2 HOURS 20 MINUTES**

This is definitely a treat on toast. The confit of garlic and tomatoes becomes sweet and sticky - a mouthwatering base for a perfectly cooked steak. The chimichurri adds some necessary freshness and a light spice!

1 garlic bulb, cloves peeled
300g (10½oz) cherry tomatoes
150–200ml (5–7fl oz) extra virgin olive oil, plus 2 tbsp
1 tbsp olive oil
2 x 275g (10oz) rump steak
2 garlic cloves, finely chopped
½ small red onion, finely chopped
1 green chilli, very finely chopped (amount used will depend on how hot your chilli is)
2 tbsp red wine vinegar
3 tbsp mayonnaise
2 tbsp finely chopped parsley
2 tbsp finely chopped coriander
2 tbsp extra virgin olive oil
flaky sea salt and freshly ground black pepper
2 extra-long pieces of sourdough, or white bread

Preheat the oven to 90°C fan (lowest setting). Put the bulb of garlic and tomatoes in a small baking tray (I like to use a wide loaf tin) so that the tomatoes fit in a single layer. Season with salt and pepper and cover with extra virgin olive oil. Put in the oven and cook for 2 hours until softened and juicy but not coloured.

Bring your steak to room temperature an hour before you want to cook, if possible.

To make the chimichurri sauce, combine the chopped garlic, onion, chilli, red wine vinegar and a pinch of salt in a bowl. Leave to sit for 10 minutes.

To prepare the steak, pat it dry with kitchen paper and season with salt and pepper. Heat a heavy-based, non-stick pan over a high heat and add the 1 tablespoon of olive oil. When hot, add the steak and cook for 2–2½ minutes on each side (for medium rare), or 3½–4 minutes on each side for well done. To render the fat side, cook this for a final 2 minutes, holding the steak in place with a pair of tongs. Set aside on a board to rest.

When the confit garlic and tomatoes are ready, put just the garlic in a bowl and mash with a fork, then add the mayonnaise.

Stir the finely chopped coriander and parsley into the chimichurri mixture. Add the 2 tablespoons of olive oil. Slice the steak lengthways, then into strips, widthways.

Spread the garlic mayonnaise onto the toast, then use a slotted spoon to transfer the cherry tomatoes over (crushing lightly with the back of the spoon). Season with black pepper. Heap the steak on top, adding any resting juices. Spoon the chimichurri over the top to finish.

Skyline

Chicken with nduja

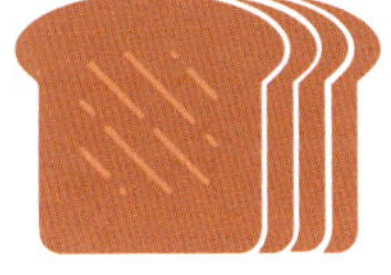

SERVES **2**

PREPARATION TIME **5 MINUTES**

COOKING TIME **15 MINUTES**

The nduja (a spicy Calabrian sausage paste) melts down here to create a deliciously rich and warming sauce for the chicken. Simple, hearty comfort food.

1 tbsp olive oil
2 boneless chicken thighs, sliced into 1cm (½in) strips
200g (7oz) cherry tomatoes, halved
3 garlic cloves, crushed
2 tbsp nduja paste
80g (3oz) sundried tomatoes, roughly chopped, plus 2 tbsp sundried tomato oil
100ml (3½fl oz) chicken stock
80g (3oz) crème fraîche
2 slices of multigrain bread

Put a large non-stick frying pan with the oil over a medium-high heat. Add the chicken and fry for 6–8 minutes until golden, then remove to a plate. Add the cherry tomatoes to the pan and fry over a high heat for a couple of minutes until they start to brown and break down. Reduce the heat and add the garlic, nduja paste and sundried tomatoes, followed by the chicken. Cook for a minute, then reduce the heat slightly and add the chicken stock. Simmer for about 10 minutes until the sauce is thickened and reduced, then remove from the heat and stir through the crème fraîche.

Toast the bread and serve the chicken and nduja mixture piled on top.

Meatball marinara

SERVES **4**

PREPARATION TIME **20 MINUTES**

COOKING TIME **25 MINUTES**

Meatballs in a thick tomato sauce, slathered in melted and golden cheese – this is peak comfort. The meatballs and sauce are great to prep ahead and then finish under the grill when ready to serve. The meatball-making is a fun activity to do with kids!

2 tbsp olive oil
1 onion, chopped
4 garlic cloves, crushed
500g (1lb 2oz) passata with basil
2 tbsp tomato purée
1 tsp caster sugar
200g (7oz) minced pork
200g (7oz) minced beef
1 tbsp Dijon mustard
5 sprigs of thyme, leaves picked and roughly chopped
25g (¾oz) parmesan, finely grated
45g (1¾oz) fresh breadcrumbs
1 egg, beaten
4 sub rolls, cut through the middle but the halves kept joined
75g (2½oz) Cheddar, grated
75g (2½oz) firm mozzarella, grated
flaky sea salt and freshly ground black pepper

Heat 1 tablespoon of olive oil in a saucepan over a medium heat. Add the onion and cook for 5–6 minutes until softened, then add half the garlic and fry for a minute before adding the passata, tomato purée and sugar. Simmer for 10 minutes.

Meanwhile, combine the minced meat, mustard, remaining garlic, thyme, parmesan, breadcrumbs and egg in a bowl. Season with salt and pepper and mix very well, then divide into 12 balls.

Heat the remaining oil in a large non-stick frying pan and place over a medium-high heat. Fry the meatballs on all sides for a total of around 7 minutes, then reduce the heat and add in the tomato sauce. Simmer for 5 minutes until the meatballs are cooked through and the sauce is thickened.

Preheat the grill to high and put the cut subs on a baking tray, then under the grill to toast. Top with the meatball mixture and then the cheese. Put under the grill until the cheese is melted and golden.

Spaghetti carbonara

SERVES **2**

PREPARATION TIME **5 MINUTES**

COOKING TIME **15 MINUTES**

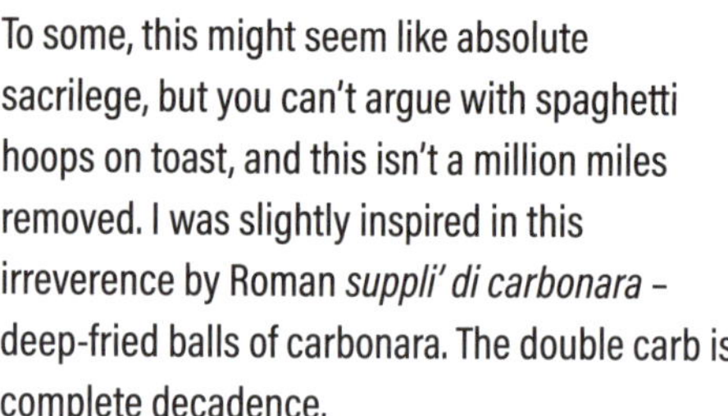

To some, this might seem like absolute sacrilege, but you can't argue with spaghetti hoops on toast, and this isn't a million miles removed. I was slightly inspired in this irreverence by Roman *suppli' di carbonara* – deep-fried balls of carbonara. The double carb is complete decadence.

100g (3½oz) spaghetti
½ tbsp olive oil
100g (3½oz) pancetta, diced, or lardons
2 garlic cloves, peeled and left whole
1 egg and 1 egg yolk, beaten together in a bowl
30g (1oz) pecorino, finely grated
30g (1oz) parmesan, finely grated, plus extra to serve
flaky sea salt and freshly ground black pepper
½ ciabatta loaf

Cook the spaghetti in boiling salted water for 1 minute less than the pack instructions. Drain, reserving a cup of pasta water.

Meanwhile, set a medium non-stick frying pan with the olive oil over a medium heat. Add the pancetta and garlic cloves and cook for 8–10 minutes until golden. Remove the garlic and reduce the heat. Add the drained spaghetti and toss to combine. Remove from the heat. Add about 6 tablespoons of pasta water, followed by the eggs and cheese, and quickly mix to combine until you have a thick, silky sauce. Season with salt and pepper. Halve the ciabatta and toast, then top with the carbonara and an extra sprinkle of cheese.

Sweet Things

Brioche with ricotta and jam

SERVES **2–4**

PREPARATION TIME **5 MINUTES**

COOKING TIME **5 MINUTES**

This is inspired by an amazing LA cafe (Sqirl) where they reinforced to me how something so simple could be so delicious! Plus ... buttery brioche fried in butter? Yes.

250g (9oz) ricotta, drained
zest of 1 orange
20g (¾oz) salted butter
4 slices of brioche
4 heaped tbsp apricot conserve

Put the ricotta in a bowl with the orange zest and mix to combine.

Heat a wide non-stick pan over a medium-high heat. Add the butter and allow to completely melt and start to bubble. Add the brioche and fry for 1–1½ minutes on each side until golden. Set aside onto plates. Generously spoon the ricotta on top, then add a heaped tablespoon of apricot conserve to the middle of each pile of ricotta.

See pages 14–15 for reference images

Amaretto roasted peaches

SERVES **4**

PREPARATION TIME **5 MINUTES**

COOKING TIME **35 MINUTES**

Stone fruits and almond go amazingly well. Almonds are actually from the same family as peach, so it's no surprise they complement each other so perfectly. The smell of roasting amaretto and caramelizing sugar – totally irresistible.

2 ripe but firm peaches, halved and pitted
3 tbsp soft light brown sugar
6 tbsp amaretto (plus extra for sauce, if needed)
125g (4oz) mascarpone
zest of 1 lemon
4 slices of brioche
50g (2oz) amaretti biscuits, roughly crushed

Preheat the oven to 180°C fan (375°F/gas 5). Put the peaches in an ovenproof dish, cut-side up. Scatter with the sugar, followed by the amaretto. Roast for 30–35 minutes until caramelized and softened.

Combine the mascarpone with the lemon zest. Toast the brioche and leave to cool for a bit. Spoon the mascarpone on top, followed by a peach half per piece. If the juices have firmed up, add an extra 1 tbsp amaretto to the pan and return to the oven for a minute or two, or place over the hob to melt. Drizzle the juices over the peach, then scatter with the crushed amaretti.

Poached pear with hazelnut butter

SERVES **4**

PREPARATION TIME **10 MINUTES**

COOKING TIME **15 MINUTES**

This is a great autumnal recipe for brunch or pudding! Perfectly poached pear, and the satisfaction of a homemade nut butter.

200ml (7fl oz) white wine
300ml (10fl oz) water
200g (7oz) golden caster sugar
pared zest of 1 lemon
2 conference pears, peeled, halved and cored
200g (7oz) blanched hazelnuts
1 tsp ground cinnamon
flaky sea salt
4 thin slices of sourdough

Combine the wine, water, caster sugar and lemon zest in a medium saucepan (big enough for the four pear halves). Set over a medium heat until the sugar has dissolved, then add the pear halves so they are submerged in the liquid. Cover with a disc of baking parchment (and weigh down slightly with a smaller pan lid which will sit on the liquid surface, just above the pears). Simmer gently for 15 minutes, then leave to cool in their liquid.

Pour 100ml (3½fl oz) of the poaching liquor into a small saucepan and return to a medium heat. Boil to reduce until you have just a third of the liquid remaining.

Meanwhile, preheat the oven to 180°C (375°/gas 5).

Toast the hazelnuts in the oven for 7–8 minutes until golden. Set 1 tablespoon of the nuts aside to be chopped, then transfer the rest straight into the small bowl of a food processor and blend until it has formed a paste (scraping down the sides intermittently to get any nuts that are escaping the blades). Add a good pinch of flaky sea salt and the cinnamon, and mix briefly to combine.

Toast the sourdough then spread with the hazelnut spread. Slice the pear and fan across each toast slice, drizzling with a little of the reduced syrup and finish with a scattering of the chopped hazelnuts.

White chocolate and pistachio paste with amarena cherries

SERVES **4**

PREPARATION TIME **5 MINUTES**

COOKING TIME **2 MINUTES**

Pistachio is one of my favourite nuts – and pistachio paste is the height of decadence. Pistachio cake ... pistachio pastries ... pistachio mochi – I'm there. This paste would be delicious as a standalone. Amarena cherries come in beautiful jars and are worth buying for that in itself, but tinned cherries also work well!

100g (3½oz) pistachios
100g (3½oz) white chocolate
80ml (3fl oz) double cream
a sprinkle of flaky sea salt
4 slices of seeded bread
4 tbsp amarena cherries, with some syrup

Put the pistachios into the small bowl of a food processor and blitz until they form a paste (be patient). Melt the white chocolate in bursts in the microwave, and bring the cream to a simmer in a small pan on the hob. With the food processor motor still running, add both the cream and the chocolate to the pistachio paste, with a sprinkle of salt flakes and mix until it makes a thick paste.

Toast the bread and then spread with the pistachio paste. Spoon the cherries on top!

Crème brûlée toast

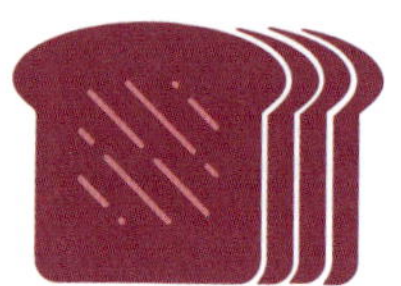

SERVES **4**

PREPARATION TIME **10 MINUTES**

COOKING TIME **20 MINUTES**

With a crust of caramelized sugar, this is a like a velveteen version of French toast. The custard stays creamy and smooth in its brioche basket, then has the crack of its sweetened topping. I served with fresh raspberries, but it would be delicious with stewed stone fruits, too.

4 slices of toasted brioche
200ml (7fl oz) double cream
3 egg yolks
1 tsp cornflour
2 tbsp caster sugar, plus 1 tbsp to serve
1 tsp vanilla bean paste
raspberries, to serve

Preheat the oven to 150°C fan (325°F/gas 3).

Use a sharp knife to remove a thin slice from the surface of each piece of brioche toast, avoiding the crusts. Arrange in a dish where the toast sits quite cosily. Put the cream into a small saucepan and bring to a gentle simmer. Meanwhile, add the egg yolks, cornflour, caster sugar and vanilla bean paste to a medium heatproof bowl and use a balloon whisk to combine. When the cream is lightly simmering, pour over the egg yolk mixture, whisking the whole time. Pour this custard mixture over the top of the bread, filling the gap in the top of the bread. Bake for 12–15 minutes, then put the dish into a larger dish of cold water to stop the cooking process. Sprinkle the remaining 1 tbsp sugar over the four pieces of toast and use a blowtorch to brûlée. Serve with raspberries on the side.

Masala chai French toast

SERVES **4**

PREPARATION TIME **10 MINUTES**

COOKING TIME **15 MINUTES**

When I tested this on my family – my guinea pigs – it was declared the most delicious French toast ... ever. I don't know If it needs any more introduction! Imbued with spice, it is warming and caramelized. I used a spiced fruit loaf for that cinnamon flavour running the whole way through, but the chai can be flavourful with a brioche bread, too.

2 English breakfast tea bags
160ml (5½fl oz) coconut cream
2 tbsp milk (dairy-free, if liked)
6 green cardamom pods, cracked open
3 tsp ground cinnamon
1 tsp ground ginger
½ tsp fennel seeds
a little grated nutmeg
1 tbsp soft brown sugar
2 eggs, beaten
8 slices of cinnamon and raisin bread
40g (1½oz) butter (salted or unsalted)
50g (2oz) caster sugar
maple syrup, for drizzling
chopped fruit, if liked

Put the tea bags into a small saucepan with the coconut cream and milk. Add the cardamom, 1 teaspoon of the cinnamon, the ginger, fennel and nutmeg with the brown sugar, then bring to a simmer. Remove from the heat and leave to brew for 10 minutes. Sieve into a bowl and beat in the eggs. Soak the bread in the egg mixture for 2½ minutes on each side (you will want to do this in batches).

Meanwhile, heat half the butter in a large non-stick frying pan over a medium-high heat until melted and beginning to bubble. Add 4 pieces of eggy toast and fry for 2 minutes on each side. Repeat with the remaining bread.

Combine the caster sugar with the remaining cinnamon in a shallow bowl. Toss the hot toast in the cinnamon sugar and serve drizzled with maple syrup and chopped fruit, if liked.

Chocolate miso spread with sesame brittle

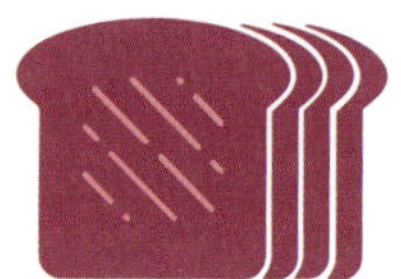

SERVES **4–6**

PREPARATION TIME **10 MINUTES**

COOKING TIME **15 MINUTES**

Rich chocolate ganache with a crunchy, salty and lightly spiced brittle – this is definitely more of a dessert toast than a sweet breakfast! The miso lends a savoury tang to the spread, and there is autumnal warmth from the light spice of the ginger and cinnamon.

40g (1½oz) sesame seeds
100g (3½oz) caster sugar
1 pinch of flaky sea salt
75g (2½oz) milk chocolate
75g (2½oz) plain chocolate
½ tsp ground cinnamon
½ tsp ground ginger
30g (1oz) butter
100ml (3½fl oz) double cream
1 ½ tbsp white miso
4–6 pieces wholegrain bread

Line a baking sheet with a piece of baking parchment. Put a large frying pan over a medium heat and add the sesame seeds and sugar to the pan and start to melt without stirring, only shaking the pan. Heat until the sugar has melted and coated the sesame seeds (you might need to encourage it with some gentle movement from a metal spoon). Carefully pour onto the baking parchment and sprinkle with a pinch of salt flakes. Set aside to cool.

Add the chocolate, spices and butter to a heatproof bowl and put over a pan of simmering water until the chocolate melts. Whisk in the cream and miso, then set aside to cool.

When the sesame brittle has cooled, break half of it into pieces and put into a high speed blender. Blitz to a dust. (Alternatively, put into a sandwich bag and smash with a rolling pin.) Stir into the chocolate ganache. Cool briefly in the fridge if you have time, until it becomes a spreadable consistency.

Toast the bread and spread with the chocolate spread. Break the remaining sesame brittle into shards and scatter on top.

Brown butter caramel bananas

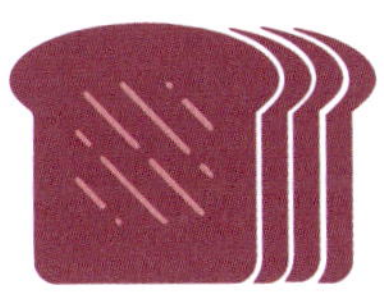

SERVES **2**

PREPARATION TIME **5 MINUTES**

COOKING TIME **15 MINUTES**

This is like a hot version of banoffee pie – the browned butter giving the sweet caramel a butterscotchy warmth. The final flourish of tahini just gives the recipe an earthy savouriness, to balance the sweet richness. Serve with wholemeal toast for a nutty undertone.

80g (3oz) butter
75g (2½oz) soft light brown sugar
5 tbsp double cream, plus 100ml (3½fl oz) for topping
2 bananas (medium ripe) cut diagonally into 6
2 slices of multiseed wholemeal bread
1 pinch of flaky sea salt
2 tbsp tahini
20g (¾oz) milk chocolate chips

Put the butter into a wide non-stick frying pan and put over a medium heat. Heat until melted, then increase the heat slightly and continue to cook until it starts to fleck with brown and smell like digestive biscuits (graham crackers) – this might take 8–10 minutes. Remove 2 tablespoons to a small bowl, and to the pan add the sugar and 5 tablespoons of cream with a pinch of flaky salt. Simmer until coming together, beating with a balloon whisk. Add the bananas and carefully toss in the caramel, then remove the pan from the heat.

Whisk the remaining cream to soft peaks. Toast the bread and top with the bananas and caramel. Top with a spoonful of cream, and drizzle with tahini. Add the reserved brown butter and scatter with chocolate chips.

Hagelslag ice-cream sandwich

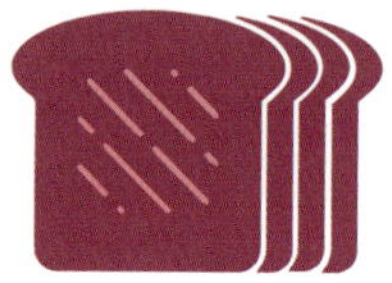

SERVES **4**

PREPARATION TIME **15 MINUTES, PLUS FREEZING**

COOKING TIME **15 MINUTES**

These are inspired by the Dutch *hagelslag* – sugared chocolate strands – which are often just eaten on buttered bread. It's not dissimilar to Australian/ Kiwi fairy bread! Straight butter on the outside of an ice cream sandwich wasn't really going so well for me, so it turned into a chocolate dip. The caramelized toast softens with the ice cream and then has a firm chocolate crust – so many layers of texture and flavour!

4 slices of medium/thin sliced white bread
45g (1¾oz) butter, softened
45g (1¾oz) light soft brown sugar
6 scoops of ice cream or sorbet (multiple flavours, if liked)
150g (5oz) plain chocolate, broken into pieces
75g (2½oz) chocolate sprinkle strands

Preheat the oven to 180°C fan (375°F/gas 5). Cut the crusts off the bread and use a rolling pin to roll as thin as possible, then cut in half (to create two rectangles per slice). Combine the butter with the soft brown sugar in a bowl and spread onto one side of each slice of bread. Lay out on a baking tray and put in the oven for 15 minutes, until caramelized. Remove to a wire rack and leave to cool for 10 minutes.

While the toast cools, bring the ice cream to room temperature. Put a piece of toast (sugared-side up) onto a square sheet of parchment. Top with some ice cream, smoothing it out carefully to the edges with a spoon. Top with a second piece of toast (sugared side facing the ice cream). Carefully push down, then wrap with the parchment. Freeze for 30 minutes, or until the ice cream is firm again. Repeat with the remaining ice cream and toast.

While the sandwiches are chilling, prepare the chocolate. Melt in bursts in a microwave or in a heatproof bowl over a pan of simmering water, then leave to cool slightly. Transfer to a mug or a jug (to make the chocolate dip as 'deep' as possible). Take the sandwiches from the freezer and dip into the chocolate. Sprinkle with sprinkles and wrap loosely again in parchment, returning to the freezer for 5 minutes to firm up.

Tiramisu

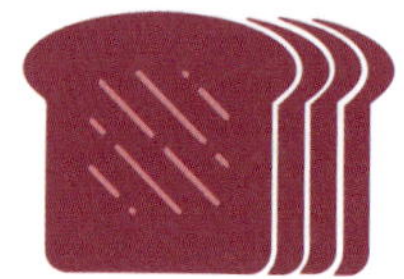

SERVES 2

PREPARATION TIME 5 MINUTES

This is a fuss-free answer to the renowned Italian dessert. With no layering or chilling, it's just five minutes' prep to bring together all the flavours that make this sweet treat so well loved!

2 thick slices of brioche or panettone
60ml (2fl oz) strong black coffee, cooled
65ml (2¼fl oz) double cream
65g (2¼oz) mascarpone
2 tbsp marsala
2 tbsp caster sugar
20g (¾oz) plain chocolate, finely grated, or 1 tsp cocoa for dusting

Toast the brioche and then spoon the espresso on slowly, allowing it to soak up the coffee before adding more. In a bowl, whisk the cream, mascarpone, marsala and sugar together until thickened and holding pillowy waves. Spoon onto the bread and scatter with the grated chocolate or cocoa.

Index

D

M

N

O

P

Acknowledgements

A big thanks to my mum and dad, who gifted me my cooking genes! Growing up and seeing them both busy in the kitchen, I always knew that food was as much about love as it was about nourishment. One evening's leftovers had the potential to be the next day's feasting – and nothing was ever wasted. This re-invention and fridge-raid mentality fed into me becoming the 'canny' cook I am today, and that inspired many of the toast-toppers in this book.

My number one taste-tester and hype boy – Justin Martin. Thank you for sampling every single dish, at all points in the day. You really let me push your limits with the number of meals I made you try, and always gave the kindest, most honest, and most enthusiastic feedback I could ask for. You're the main reason I believe I can achieve anything, with my work and with life.

To Heather Boisseau and Matt Tomlinson – thank you to the moon for the chance to author my own book! I couldn't believe my eyes when this opportunity landed in my inbox and felt so incredibly lucky throughout the journey of writing and styling the book. The fact that I get to cook for a living still sometimes stops me in my tracks. This book has been a joy.

Simon Smith and Simon Reed – the photo shoot was a blast and the photography does amazing justice to a fantastic selection of recipes (even if I do say so myself). I loved our shoot lunches and seeing everyone carb-load on my creations. Max Robinson – the props were all gorgeous, and thank you for such stylish attention to detail. You're a genius. And to my incredibly hard-working and diligent assistants, Jess Geddes and Maria Gurevich – always thank you. Knowing that you enjoyed the recipes gave me so much reassurance and pride, and I couldn't have done any of it without you both!

Picture credits

Shutterstock An Vin, 4; MM Memo, 10–1, 46, 72–3, 120, 148; roughedges_stock 24–5, 92–3.